# ANALECTA GORGIANA

Volume 19

General Editor

## George Anton Kiraz

*Analecta Gorgiana* is a collection of long essays and short monographs which are consistently cited by modern scholars but previously difficult to find because of their original appearance in obscure publications. Now conveniently published, these essays are not only vital for our understanding of the history of research and ideas, but are also indispensable tools for the continuation and development of on-going research. Carefully selected by a team of scholars based on their relevance to modern scholarship, these essays can now be fully utilized by scholars and proudly owned by libraries.

# The Day and Year of
Saint Polycarp's Martyrdom

# The Day and Year of Saint Polycarp's Martyrdom

C. H. Turner

Gorgias Press
2006

First Gorgias Press Edition, 2006

The special contents of this edition are copyright © 2006 by
Gorgias Press LLC

All rights reserved under International and Pan-American Copyright
Conventions. Published in the United States of America by
Gorgias Press LLC, New Jersey

This edition is a facsimile reprint of the
original edition published in *Studia Biblica et Ecclesiastica*,
Oxford, 1890, vol. 2.

*Analecta Gorgiana* pagination appears in square brackets.

ISBN 1-59333-497-4

GORGIAS PRESS
46 Orris Ave., Piscataway, NJ 08854 USA
www.gorgiaspress.com

The paper used in this publication meets the minimum requirements of the
American National Standards.

Printed in the United States of America

# THE DAY AND YEAR OF St. POLYCARP'S MARTYRDOM[1].

### C. H. TURNER

Μαρτυρεῖ δὲ ὁ μακάριος πολύκαρπος μηνὸς ξανθικοῦ δευτέρᾳ ἱσταμένου, πρὸ ἑπτὰ καλανδῶν μαρτίων, σαββάτῳ μεγάλῳ, ὥρᾳ ὀγδόῃ· συνελήφθη ὑπὸ ἡρώδου ἐπὶ ἀρχιερέως φιλίππου τραλλιανοῦ, ἀνθυπατεύοντος στατίου κοδράτου, βασιλεύοντος δὲ εἰς τοὺς αἰῶνας ἰησοῦ χριστοῦ· ᾧ ἡ δόξα, τιμή, μεγαλωσύνη, θρόνος αἰώνιος ἀπὸ γενεᾶς εἰς γενεάν. ἀμήν.

THE readers of this volume of *Studia Biblica* will not unnaturally ask why, in presence of the very numerous questions which might reasonably demand notice in our sphere of work, one so apparently trivial as the exact date of a martyrdom should require to be re-opened for a fresh discussion after the learned and exhaustive paper read before the Society by Mr. Randell, of St. John's, in February, 1884, and printed in the earlier number of the series of which the present publication is the second.

To this question two answers may be offered.

In the first place, on the general ground it may be asserted that, minute as the enquiry doubtless is, there are few problems in the Christian history of the second century of equal interest and of equal importance with the precise dating of St. Polycarp's death. It is not only that it is a pivot of ecclesiastical chronology, but that on it depends largely the value we can place on the succession St. John, Polycarp, Irenaeus. Irenaeus was born not later, probably earlier, than

---

[1] An abstract of this paper has already appeared in print in the *Guardian* for April 18, 1888; and the writer takes this opportunity of thanking the Editor for his courtesy in consenting to what is more or less a republication of it.

A.D. 130. St. John lived on in Asia Minor down to the close of the first century. Between them stands Polycarp, and it is on the chronological proof of his intercourse with each of them that the issue turns. For Polycarp was eighty-six years old at the time of his martyrdom (*Mart. Pol.* § ix), and thus, after covering the at most thirty years' interval between the death of St. John and the birth of Irenaeus, more than half a century of his life remains which, if anything like equally divided between the life-time of his teacher and the life-time of his pupil, is amply sufficient to warrant him a trustworthy link between the one and the other. But when we fix the martyrdom of St. Polycarp, we fix also his birth, and therewith the length of his possible connection alike with his successor and with his predecessor.

It needs no more to show the intrinsic importance of the enquiry. But even so the re-opening of it here would be scarcely in place, were it not that the present writer—and this must be his main defence—is in a position of great advantage as compared with Mr. Randell, both because the latter's paper is ready to his hand, and even more by the intermediate appearance of the Bishop of Durham's volumes on St. Ignatius and St. Polycarp; not the least exhaustive or least conclusive portion of that memorable work being the discussion (vol. i. pp. 610-702) of the date of the martyrdom in question [1].

When Mr. Randell wrote there was, it is true, already a general tendency among English scholars as well as on the Continent to admit the soundness of the arguments with which M. Waddington had sought, by the aid of a reconsideration of the chronological notices given in the rhetorician Aelius Aristides, to fix the date of the Asiatic proconsulship of T. Statius Quadratus—under whom, according to the

---

[1] All references in these pages are to the first edition of Bishop Lightfoot's work unless otherwise stated: the new edition (1889) came to hand too late to be employed in the text, and I have therefore added to my appendices a note on the new matter introduced, and especially on the criticism he has done me the honour to devote to my own view.

notices of the Letter of the Church of Smyrna (known as the *Martyrium Polycarpi*) the saint undoubtedly suffered—not, as had hitherto been the case, to the reign of Marcus Aurelius (A.D. 161–180), but to that of his predecessor Antoninus Pius (A.D. 138–161). Aristides dates events both by proconsuls and by the years of a certain malady to which he was long subject, and so, if we can find external evidence for the date of any one proconsul who is mentioned in this connection, we could then argue by the years of the malady to other proconsuls similarly introduced. Now Julianus was, says Aristides, proconsul a year and some months after the malady commenced, and an inscription fixes this proconsulship to A.D. 145. From Julianus we get to Severus, from Severus to Quadratus, who is in consequence usually placed in A.D. 154–155 [1].

But there were then still those who held to the traditional view. Among ourselves, Bishop Chr. Wordsworth, in his latest work (cf. *A Church History to the Council of Nicaea,* 1881, p. 161, note [2]), held it, though hesitatingly; and in Germany, Keim, a writer of by no means conservative tendencies, was equally unconvinced. Now, however, by the labours of Bishop Lightfoot, the question may almost be said, at least in England, to have been set at rest. Whatever doubt may have hung over the reconstructed Aristidean chronology, when that reconstruction stood alone, has surely been dis-

---

[1] However, since the proconsuls held office, not from January to January, but from May to May, and because of the impossibility of arguing from one date to another without leaving a certain margin, more cannot be claimed with certainty for the ultimate result (as Dr. Lightfoot admits, p. 650), than that Quadratus came into office not earlier than A.D. 153, and not later than A.D. 155, so that the martyrdom can so far fall anywhere between May A.D. 153 and May A.D. 156; and though both the writers whose investigation into the details of this subject gives them the best claim to be heard, Waddington and Lightfoot, place the martyrdom early in A.D. 155, there are not wanting critics of the first rank, such as Hilgenfeld and Lipsius (see below), who on one ground or another prefer to place it early in A.D. 156.

[2] But in the latest edition (1889) the note in question has been re-written, 'in accordance with a request made by' the late Bishop before his death to the present Bishop of Salisbury. See below, note, p. 152.

sipated by the striking coincidence with it of the epigraphical evidence relative to the date of another official mentioned in the account of the martyrdom. As the first discussion started from the name of the Proconsul, Quadratus, so the later discoveries centre round the name of the Asiarch, Philip of Tralles (*Mart. Pol.* §§ 12, 21). From one Trallian inscription we learn that the Trallian games of the 'eighth Olympiad after the Restoration' took place shortly before the death of Antoninus, probably late in A.D. 160 or early in A.D. 161. The 'Restoration' must therefore have happened about thirty years beforehand, and was doubtless reckoned from Hadrian's visit to Asia Minor in A.D. 129, so that the first Olympiad would probably begin in A.D. 129, and the eighth in A.D. 157. Hence we can also fix the fifty-sixth Olympiad, if, as seems the case, that is only a magniloquent paraphrase for the sixth, to A.D. 149–153; and the fifty-sixth is mentioned in two inscriptions in connection with the Trallian games held under G. Julius Philippus, who was simultaneously 'High-Priest of Asia.' This interpretation is confirmed by a further inscription from Olympia, which speaks of Philip of Tralles as Asiarch in the 232nd Olympiad, that is, some time in A.D. 149–152. These two results so entirely coincide that no hesitation need be felt in concluding that Philip of Tralles was Asiarch somewhere in the years A.D. 150–152. Then since the Asiarchate, like the periodical games, was 'pentaeteric,' that is renewed every four years, it may either be supposed that Philip was re-elected for a second tenure of office, or more simply that he was originally elected in A.D. 151 or 152, and so did not vacate till A.D. 155 or 156. These conclusions are worked out by the Bishop of Durham (pp. 612–618, cf. ii. 987–998), and this close agreement of two independent lines of evidence to the central years of the decade, A.D. 150–160, seemed to remove any possibility of scepticism [1].

[1] One or two suggestions may be added in completion of the Bishop's argument. Since the Asiatic year began in September (see inf. p. 113) it may be presumed that the 'Restoration' Olympiads date from September A.D. 129, and

## of St. Polycarp's Martyrdom.

Before, however, dismissing for good the older view, which connected the martyrdom with the reign of Marcus, it will be worth while to examine for one moment the grounds on which it was based. In this, as in so many other chronological matters, it is pretty clear that later writers[1] have

the sixth or fifty-sixth would not end till September A.D. 153, nor the eighth till September A.D. 161. Again, if Trallian games occurred shortly before Antoninus' death in March 161 A.D., then since they were no doubt pentaeteric, the other inscriptions relating to victories in the Trallian games two Olympiads earlier, may be fixed with great probability near the early months of A.D. 153. Future epigraphic discoveries may, one cannot help surmising, give us substantial help in this sort of way towards the Polycarpian question.

[1] Thus Jerome (*De Vir. Illustr.* 17) mentions Polycarp's visit to Anicetus as under Antoninus Pius, his martyrdom as under 'M. Antoninus' and L. Aurelius Commodus; apparently following Eusebius, *H. E.* iv. 14, 15, where the visit is mentioned before, the martyrdom after, the accession of 'Marcus Aurelius Verus, who is also Antoninus.'

The Church historian Socrates is, however, a strange exception, for in his well-known chapter on diversities of usage in different Churches (*H. E.* v. 22, p. 238, Bright), he instances the Quartodeciman dispute, and in connection with it the visit to Anicetus of Polycarp, ὃ καὶ ὕστερον ἐπὶ Γορδιανοῦ μαρτυρήσας, that is between A.D. 238 and A.D. 244! The only point of interest in so extraordinary a blunder is the question how can it have arisen, especially as Socrates is a more than usually careful writer, and ordinarily follows Eusebius closely; indeed, the visit to Anicetus, which is the only motive for the introduction of Polycarp's name here at all, is taken from the earlier historian (though from *H. E.* v. 24, not iv. 14). It would be natural to suppose that he would have turned to Eusebius for the date of the martyrdom as well, if he had not believed himself to have other quite trustworthy authority for his statement. Either then he confused the great Polycarp with one of the other martyrs of the same name, to whose existence the oldest Kalendars witness (cf. Lightfoot, i. p. 689, Syriac K. under Jan. 27, Latin K. under Feb. 23); or, if he had, as is not unlikely, the martyrium at his command (§ 21 μαρτυρεῖ δὲ ὁ μακάριος Πολύκαρπος . . . ἐπὶ ἀρχιερέως Φιλίππου Τραλλιανοῦ ἀνθυπατεύοντος Στατίου Κοδράτου), the conjecture may be offered that the phrase 'in the highpriesthood of Philip the Trallian,' occurring before the Proconsul, in the place where the mention of the Emperor might be anticipated, may have originated the error. Ἀρχιερέως would be read αὐτοκρατόρος, or interpreted of the Emperor as Pontifex Maximus; and ΤΡΑΛ-ΛΙΑΝΟΥ appears in some MSS. as ΤΡΑΙΑΝΟΥ, the *ductus litterarum* of which is sufficiently near to ΓοΡΔΙΑΝΟΥ. Philip and Gordian were apparently for a time colleagues in the empire; but as Philip was believed to have been a Christian, Socrates would repeat only Gordian's name as the persecutor. Or, an alternative explanation might be, that since a Philip is commemorated on coins as Recorder of Tralles in the age of the Gordians (Lightfoot, p. 960) the Asiarch Philip had in some way got confused with his later homonym, and been assigned his date.

only followed the fashion set by Eusebius, who in his *History* (iv. 15) inserts the Martyrium, or the greater part of it, immediately after the notice of Antoninus' death, and in his *Chronicle* was believed to have found a more precise date in A.D. 166 or 167. But in the latter passage, as Dr. Lightfoot, never more felicitous than when dealing with Eusebius, has conclusively shown, the historian is merely grouping together at some convenient point in this reign, as he has done in other reigns, all notices of persecutions belonging to it, but not otherwise dated. There is nothing really to suggest that for his Chronicle he possessed more detailed knowledge than is given in the History, where he even includes in the comparatively small omissions from the Martyrium the concluding section, teeming though it does with notices of time, each of which has contributed something to the modern enquiry, while none of them could have enlightened a writer destitute of our modern collections of provincial Fasti, lists of local Kalendars, and *Corpora* of inscriptions. Eusebius can in fact only be quoted as a witness to the *reign*, not to the *year*, of the martyrdom ; and if we ask why he selected the reign of Pius rather than that of Marcus, it is plain that where the Martyrium itself failed to help him, he must have been thrown back on other and more general indications.

Such would be, primarily, the visit of Polycarp to Anicetus of Rome, our only piece of independent external evidence, twice quoted by Eusebius from Irenaeus (*H. E.* iv. 14, v. 24). Since the Episcopate of Anicetus is reckoned in the History as lasting from A.D. 157 to 168 [1], and since Marcus succeeded to the throne early in A.D. 161, it was clear that there were more chances than not that, if not the visit, at any rate the martyrdom would fall under him. This conclusion would be

---

[1] Similarly Jerome's version of the Chronicle. The Armenian version does not essentially differ at this point; in any case see Lightfoot, ii. pp. 461–465, where Dr. Hort supplies good reasons for rejecting the common view that the Armenian correctly represents the original Chronicle—a view which necessitates the improbable hypothesis that Eusebius in his two works had two different chronologies of the Roman Bishops.

in accord with Eusebius' *parti pris* concerning the relation of the two Emperors to Christianity. According to him Pius was no persecutor, while Marcus confessedly was. On the one hand, the (spurious) toleration edict of *H. E.* iv. 13 is beyond question understood by Eusebius (whether rightly or wrongly) as belonging to Antoninus: and Melito's *Apology*, quoted in iv. 26, distinctly speaks of letters of the same Emperor to different cities in the Christian interest. On the other, he saw that the context in Melito postulates an existing persecution under Marcus, and the story of the Martyrs of Lyons (*H. E.* v. 1) belongs to the same reign [1].

Beyond doubt, then, Eusebius, if he had no other means of distinguishing, would have selected the reign of Marcus for the martyrdom of Polycarp on these *a priori* grounds, and the value of his evidence is neither more nor less than the probabilities of their correctness. But the presumptions on which, in the absence of other data, it was necessary for him to argue are nothing in face of the more definite evidence obtained from Aristides and the inscriptions; and the soundness of the conclusion of Waddington and Lightfoot is therefore established negatively as well as positively.

But if it is thus certain that the true date falls in or near A.D. 155, it is natural to ask further whether there is no means which will enable us to fix more exactly the year and even the day of the martyrdom; and the answer to the question lies in the Chronological Postscript to the Martyrium which is printed at the head of this paper. 'The Blessed

[1] One indeed of Eusebius' authorities, the *Apologeticus* of Tertullian, which he knew in a Greek translation (*H. E.* ii. 3, iii. 33), claimed all the good Emperors, and among them of course both Antoninus and Aurelius—but the latter, on the strength of the story of the Thundering Legion, with special emphasis—as protectors of the Christians. But Eusebius (erroneously) referred the Legion legend, and the consequent epistle of 'Marcus, the understanding Emperor,' to Aurelius' brother L. Verus, quoting Tertullian as an authority (*H. E.* v. 5); and either Tertullian's Greek translator (who certainly took the liberty to re-arrange Tertullian's haphazard mention of Emperors into chronological order: cf. *Apol.* 5 with *H. E.* v. 5), or more probably Eusebius himself significantly omitted the mention of 'Verus' (i. e. M. Aurelius) in the catalogue of non-persecuting Emperors.

Polycarp is martyred on the second of the month Xanthicus, the seventh before the Kalends of March, on a high Sabbath, at the eighth hour; he was arrested by Herod, Philip of Tralles being high priest, and Statius Quadratus proconsul.' Of these indications the last two, the Proconsulship and the Asiarchate have been already spoken of. There remain four, the day and month in the Asiatic reckoning; the same in the Roman reckoning; the day of the week; and the 'high' or festal character of the day. It is in this second part of the discussion that the treatment by Bishop Lightfoot is so unique in its thoroughness as necessarily to supply the material and the model for every subsequent writer. Only those who should compare the rest of this paper, paragraph by paragraph, and line by line, with the corresponding sections of the great work on which it is built, would understand how extensive and far-reaching the obligation is; and one is almost ashamed to feel that one has employed the matter so copiously supplied only in the construction of an alternative hypothesis.

(1) *The Roman day and month*: πρὸ ἑπτὰ καλανδῶν Μαρτίων, i.e. a. d. vii Kal. Mart., or February 23rd.

(2) *The Asiatic day and month*: μηνὸς Ξανθικοῦ δευτέρᾳ ἱσταμένου, the 2nd of Xanthicus. To help us in an enquiry into the Asiatic Kalendar of Imperial times we have (a) a 'Hemerologium of the months of different cities,' arranged to show the relation of each to the official Julian Kalendar of Rome, and preserved in two MSS., respectively at Florence and at Leyden; among the kalendars given being more than one of the Asiatic group [1]: (b) three inscriptions of Proconsular Asia, which give side by side the Roman and the native dating, one of them as early as B.C. 1, the second of A.D. 104, and the third as late as 'the age of the Antonines'; this last from Smyrna itself [2]. The evidence of these two sources, MS.

---

[1] See *Histoire de l'Academie Royale des Inscriptions et Belles-Lettres*, tom. 47, pp. 66–84 (1809).

[2] But see also the appendices to this paper, where important additional material is adduced.

and inscriptions, is completely harmonious; and its general results may be summed up as follows.

The object of the introduction of such a kalendar—it dates from very shortly before the Christian era—would be, with as little change as possible in familiar names, such as those of the months, to arrive at some intelligible fixed relation with the universal and official kalendar of Rome. It must therefore of course be solar, while the older kalendar had been lunar; and further, though no change was introduced into the *names* of the months, which still differ in different cities, their relation to the Roman (that is practically to our own) Kalendar was the same throughout Proconsular Asia. Everywhere the year begins, not in midwinter, but at the autumnal equinox; everywhere the months begin eight days before the corresponding Roman months, and each has thus as many days as the Roman month with which it for the most part coincides. These peculiarities of the Kalendar are a sign and an outcome of the extraordinary pitch to which Caesar-worship was carried from the very first in Asia. September 23rd (a. d. ix Kal. Oct.) was the birthday of Augustus; not only was the year made to begin on this day, but every month began likewise on the ninth before the Kalends, so as to give, besides the yearly, a monthly commemoration of the birthday on the first of every month. A further point to be remembered in this Asian Kalendar is, that the 31st was never used; in months of thirty-one days the 1st was repeated, so that the really second day was also called the 1st, the real third the 2nd, and so on till the month ended with a real thirty-first called the 30th: or to put it otherwise, a day was intercalated at the commencement of every such month.

Xanthicus was one of the Macedonian names for the months; but these were at this time used by two kalendars, and in the Syro-Macedonian Kalendar of Josephus, Eusebius, and the Apostolic Constitutions the months are one ahead of the Asio-Macedonian. So in Syria Xanthicus is the seventh month or April, in Asia the sixth, and roughly equivalent to

March[1]. Commencing then with a. d. ix Kal. Mart. (Feb. 21), and since March is a month of thirty-one days repeating its first, the second Xanthicus is Feb. 23, or a. d. vii Kal. Mart., as given in the Martyrium.

(3) *The day of the week*: σαββάτῳ, Sabbath or Saturday.

The two results first obtained, though confirming one another and independently witnessing to Feb. 23 as the day and month of the martyrdom, fail to help us to the year. But when we add to these a third in the day of the week, we can proceed to ask in which of the possible years 154, 155, 156 A.D. did Feb. 23 fall on a Saturday, and it is found by calculation that it was in A.D. 155. Feb. 23, 155 A.D., is therefore the year and day for which Dr. Lightfoot concludes.

(4) *The feast*: σαββάτῳ μεγάλῳ, 'a high sabbath.'

Beyond doubt this feast was a Jewish one: the only possible Christian high sabbath would be the Saturday before the Pascha, which, at least among Quartodecimans, would itself coincide with the great Jewish feast. But about the time we require, the end of February, there is one and only one important feast, the Jewish Purim, exactly the occasion, with its memories of Esther and Mordecai, to rouse Jewish popular excitement as we hear it was roused against Polycarp. Now Purim was held at the full moon of Adar (the month before Nisan), that is, since the Jewish months began with the new moon, on Adar 14, 15; and according to Jewish use a 'high sabbath' connected with it will be the sabbath *previous* to the 14th[2]. The 'high sabbath' of the modern Jews is the sabbath

---

[1] The origin of this curious variation lay, it is natural to suppose, in the difficulty of the transformation of lunar into solar months. To take a familiar instance, the Jewish month Nisan (for which Josephus uses Xanthicus as the secular equivalent) being that whose full moon fell first after the spring equinox, might in some years be nearly equivalent to the Roman solar month March, in others to April, and thus if Nisan had to be Romanized, it might have been turned into either of the two.

[2] This sort of use, the reverse of our own system of keeping an Octave on the Sunday after a great festival, has its survival or counterpart in the Kalendar of the Eastern Church, where Quinquagesima week, for instance, is the week before, not the week after Quinquagesima; see Burgon, *Last Twelve Verses of St. Mark*, p. 194.

before the Passover, and the Roman Jews of the present day keep the sabbath before Pentecost as *a* 'high sabbath.' On the high authority of Dr. Neubauer it may be added that the Jews of the second century may not improbably have similarly kept the sabbath before Purim.

But what relation did the Jewish feast of Purim bear in A.D. 155 to Feb. 23?

In that year the first full moon after Feb. 23 fell about March 7, so that even if that were (as no doubt it was) the full moon of Adar, yet since Purim would be about March 6 and 7, the 'high sabbath' before it must have been not Saturday, Feb. 23, but Saturday, March 2 [1]. What is to be said to this?

Dr. Lightfoot's answer would simply be, that the Jewish Kalendar of the second century was in a state of such confusion, that it would be hopeless to fix Purim, or the 'high sabbath' before the feast, by its means. Any feast might fall anywhere at all near its true time; and as the rest of the evidence seemed to point conclusively to Feb. 23, 155 A.D., he assumes that Purim must have occurred simultaneously, and has not investigated this branch of the question. But has not the Bishop exaggerated the extent to which confusion was possible in a lunar kalendar like the Jewish?

There are two natural divisions of time, the lunar month or the time from new to new moon, averaging 29½ days, and the solar year, or succession of the seasons regulated by the sun, nearly equal to 365 days; and these two are the base respectively of the genuine lunar and solar kalendars. Both the month and year, however, are convenient divisions of time,

---

[1] If the discrepancy had been only one of a day or two, it might have been feasible to conceive hypotheses in explanation of it. But the one main qualification possible for the statement in the text tells the other way, for so far as the Jewish Kalendar was still based on observation, the first of the month must fall a day or so after the astronomical new moon, and the fifteenth similarly later than the true full moon. That is to say, in A.D. 155, Purim may have been still later than March 6 and 7, and February 23 falls still more decisively out of the question.

and therefore each of the two kalendars borrowed the distinctive time-division of its rival. In particular the Jewish Kalendar was from the first that we know of it in the Pentateuch a combination of this sort. Lunar, because its months were lunar, each beginning with the new moon, it was yet in practice solar as well, for the feasts of unleavened bread, of harvest, and of ingathering (Exod. xxiii. 15, 16) are connected with the cycle of the seasons. Obviously the attempt would soon be made to reduce the year and the months to a common denomination; in other words, from the moment that these solar feasts were fixed to definite months (Exod. xii. 2, 6, xiii. 4, Deut. xvi. 1, 9, etc.) it followed that the months themselves, which were lunar, must be brought into some relation with the solar year. Now it is easy enough for ourselves to correlate our months and year, because our months are only artificial divisions of the solar year, approximating to, but not identical with, the true month. The difference indeed between the lunar month and the twelfth of the solar year is comparatively minute (about a day), but twelve lunar months, instead of making 365, make only 354 days; and this divergence would of course very soon increase so far as to destroy all relation with the solar year, and therewith all connection of definite months with the feasts of definite seasons of the year. The device which the Jews employed, no doubt at an early time, as we know they did later, was simply the intercalation of a thirteenth month whenever the twelfth ended too soon for the offerings of the firstfruits of the barley harvest, which marked the feast of unleavened bread (Deut. xvi. 9, Lev. xxiii. 10), to be made in the middle of the next month at the full moon of Nisan [1]. As the twelve lunar months fall short of the solar year by eleven days, this would happen on an average rather oftener than once in three years.

It is, however, to be remembered that in both directions the original Jewish Kalendar was formed on the principles, not of

---

[1] Cf. *Dictionary of the Bible*, iii. p. 1804, article 'Year,' by Mr. R. S. Poole.

calculation, but of observation; the month began when the moon was seen to be new, the year when the barley harvest was approaching ripeness, and no serious mistakes were possible. The system was free from complexity, but suitable only to a people living in an area so small (the Holy Land is not more than about the size of Wales) that the beginning of the coming month could be fixed at Jerusalem for all Palestine the day before. The difficulty indeed in the case of the months cannot have been great, even after the Dispersion, for the new moon would be usually visible on the same evening throughout the eastern shores of the Mediterranean, and anyone could perform the operation of observing it for himself. But the commencement of the year, involving the question of the intercalation of a thirteenth month, stood on different ground. It was impossible for a Jew of Mesopotamia or of Egypt to tell by observation when the barley harvest would be ripe in Palestine, and therefore in what month he was wanted at Jerusalem for the Passover. That could be fixed only on the spot, and the knowledge would have to be communicated to foreign Jews in time to allow of their arrival before the middle of the first month Nisan—an obviously impracticable feat. Therefore as soon as (if not before) the Jews of the Dispersion had to be taken into account as well as those of Palestine, the old empiric methods must have given place to some system of universal application. Instead then of the first ripe ears of barley harvest, the spring equinox seems to have become at some unknown period the *terminus a quo* of the Paschal full moon—the limit before which the middle of the first month Nisan might not fall—and in this way the ultimate starting-point of the Jewish Kalendar. Some such reform, even if never made before, would have become a literal necessity when the destruction of the Temple put an end to the central worship, and each community had to keep the Passover for itself. With the disappearance of the single celebration, and of the authority which regulated it, unity had for the future to be sought in the adoption of a single self-perpetuating kalendar. But the commencement of the new year according to the equinox was not a simple matter of astronomical observation like the new moon of the month; for (not to speak of the different dates assigned to the equinox) it was not the new moon but the full moon only of Nisan which had to fall after it, while the intercalation of a month, when necessary, would have to be determined upon some weeks earlier still. Therefore, just as the Christians found with their Easter, so the Jews with their Passover doubtless felt that the only means to secure uniformity was the universal adoption of some cycle based on astronomical calculations for a long sequence of years which should show the day of the Passover for each year, and, like a recurring series of decimals, should begin again as soon as it was finished, with the same dates. Ultimately the Jews resorted unanimously to the nineteen years' cycle. But that was long after the era of St. Polycarp. In the second century, what with the various equinoxes and rival cycles and independent observations, the Jewish Kalendar was apparently in a state of hopeless confusion.

Only, while all this is perfectly true, it will be noticed at once that the whole perplexity was concerned with the year, and with the months only in their relation to the year, not in themselves. Least of all does it cover Dr. Lightfoot's hypothesis that the Jews ever celebrated a full moon feast such as that of Purim in Adar—and if Purim in Adar, why not Passover in Nisan?—at any other time than that of full moon when the veriest tyro's observation of the heavens would prove them in the wrong[1]. And there is the further presumption against it, that had so gross a mistake in the

---

[1] If anything could make disagreement with Dr. Lightfoot on such a point less burdensome, it would be agreement with Dr. Salmon, and it is therefore encouraging to find that the latter writer, in the article *Polycarp* in the last volume of the Dictionary of Christian Biography (vol. iv. p. 430, cols. 1, 2, note), while admitting that his own hypothesis had been disproved by the Bishop, makes the same criticism on the Bishop's theory as has been made here.

Paschal calculations ever occurred, we should surely have heard of it, if not from Jewish, at any rate from Christian sources. The Asiatic Church of St. Polycarp's day kept its Pascha with the Jews and hotly contested the view that the Christian celebration was to be connected with the day of the week rather than with the day of the month; yet they were never accused of mistaking the true fourteenth, and indeed even their adversaries started from the same fourteenth and reckoned the Sunday after it as their festival. Again, when at the beginning of the third century the Christians found out with their greater astronomical knowledge that the Jewish methods were deficient (so that their superior science combined with their growing hatred of Judaism in inducing them to strike out a new line for themselves) they have their definite gravamen against the Jews, but it is connected with the calculation, not of the month, but of the year. 'They often celebrate the Passover,' it was said [1], 'twice in the same year,' counting, that is, from equinox to equinox. In other words, the Jewish 15th Nisan did not always fall, as it should have done, after the equinox, and when it wrongly fell before, it was the second Passover held since the March equinox of the preceding year. There was no question either then or earlier of a mistake of anything less than a month. The Passover and similarly Purim (as another full moon feast) might be a month wrong, as being held at the wrong full moon; but they could only be a month wrong. An error of a fortnight, the celebration of the full moon at the new moon, is

---

[1] Cf. the Letter of Constantine to the Churches from the Council of Nicaea (in Socrates, $H. E.$ i. 9, p. 24, Bright): μηδὲν τοίνυν ἔστω ὑμῖν κοινὸν μετὰ τοῦ ἐχθίστου τῶν Ἰουδαίων ὄχλου ... κἂν τούτῳ τῷ μέρει τὴν ἀλήθειαν οὐχ ὁρῶσιν, ὡς ἀεὶ κατὰ τὸ πλεῖστον αὐτοὺς πλανωμένους, ἀντὶ τῆς προσηκούσης ἐπανορθώσεως, ἐν τῷ αὐτῷ ἔτει δεύτερον τὸ Πάσχα ἐπιτελεῖν. So again the Apostolic Constitutions (v. 17, p. 149 Lagarde) δεῖ οὖν ὑμᾶς, ἀδελφοί ... τὰς ἡμέρας τοῦ Πάσχα ἀκριβῶς ποιεῖσθαι μετὰ πάσης ἐπιμελείας μετὰ τροπὴν ἰσημερίνην, ὅπως μὴ δὶς τοῦ ἐνιαυτοῦ ἑνὸς παθήματος μνείαν ποιῆσθε ... μηκέτι παρατηρούμενοι μετὰ Ἰουδαίων ἑορτάζειν ... πεπλάνηνται γὰρ καὶ αὐτὴν τὴν ψηφόν, κ.τ.λ. The same seems to be the drift of an earlier writer, Anatolius of Laodicea, a passage of whose Κανόνες περὶ τοῦ Πάσχα is preserved in Eusebius, $H. E.$ vii. 32.

inconceivable; an error of a week little less so. Dr. Lightfoot's hypothesis requires an error of at least four or five days [1].

It seems therefore to have been proved satisfactorily that Saturday, Feb. 23, A.D. 155, is the only possible day, and yet that it fails to satisfy an important condition. Is there no way out of the difficulty?

The thought suggested itself that in the next year, A.D. 156, Nisan 15 would fall about March 24, and Adar 15 or Purim about February 24 [2], as the year was leap-year. But then of course as Feb. 23 was Saturday in A.D. 155, not Feb. 23 but Feb. 22 should be Saturday in A.D. 156, and the 'high sabbath' before Purim. We seem therefore equally at fault here, for the condition 'the seventh before the Kalends of March' is not satisfied.

But it is not inopportune to draw attention now to the fact that the primary datum is the 2nd Xanthicus, which is only explained as being the seventh before the Kalends, or Feb. 23. Was there then no possible means by which at least in A.D. 156, Xanthicus 2 might really fall on the *eighth* before the Kalends, Saturday, February 22?

It is here that the most curious phenomenon of the investigation meets us. Lightfoot gives four inscriptions as the only instances with double Asiatic and Roman dating; one of these, an Ephesian inscription of A.D. 104, is dated on the '2nd of Anthesterion,' the very same day as that of Polycarp's martyrdom (for Anthesterion is the Athenian and Ephesian name for Xanthicus) and the equivalent given is, *not the seventh, but the eighth* before the March Kalends, Feb. 22: πρὸ

---

[1] Dr. Neubauer, whose kindness I gratefully acknowledge, answers me that a day's error is as much as need be taken into account.

[2] In years where a month is intercalated, Adar is of course not the month next before, but next but one before Nisan. Happily this special source of confusion may be left out of account, as in neither of the years A.D. 155 or 156 was an intercalation necessary.

The astronomical dates are given in the text; it has been already mentioned that, if the new moon was fixed by observation, dates at least a day later must be given for the full moon feasts: but the argument is not affected.

## of St. Polycarp's Martyrdom.

η' καλανδῶν Μαρτίων... 'Ανθεστηριῶνος β' σεβαστῇ[1]. The coincidence is singularly striking; and if we may provisionally assume Feb. 22 for St. Polycarp's day, the two support one another, though the anomaly, even if a double one, still requires explanation, for certainly the Asiatic Kalendar was older than A.D. 104, and lived on as late as A.D. 156, and in the Asiatic Kalendar Xanthicus 2 was Feb. 23. In the case of the inscription Dr. Lightfoot supposes that the Asiatic 'double 1st' was not employed; but if not necessary at Ephesus in A.D. 104, why should it be necessary at Smyrna in A.D. 156? Here would be one defence of the date now offered, Feb. 22, A.D. 156[2].

But a hint worth working out is supplied by Dr. Lightfoot in calling attention to the use, in the inscription mentioned, of the word σεβαστῇ, which is used of a day of the month only in three inscriptions from Egypt—two of them simply Θωὺθ σεβαστῇ and Φαρμοῦθ σεβαστῇ, but the third Φαωφὶ α' 'Ιουλίᾳ σεβαστῇ—and in the Leyden MS. of the Hemerology already referred to, where it stands opposite the first day of several months in the Lycian Kalendar. Clearly there is some connection between σεβαστή, Augustus' day, and the first of the month. May it not be then a sort of monthly commemoration of the Emperor on the prerogative day of each month, so that the Asiatics will have outdone their neighbours, not by a monthly commemoration of Augustus on the first, which was more widely observed, but by the unique compliment of making this commemoration coincide with his actual birthday, the ninth before the Kalends? But then the σεβαστὴ is added only to some of the Lycian months. True; to those only of thirty-one days. As Usener says—the point of whose reasoning on this subsidiary question Dr. Lightfoot seems not to have quite reproduced—there is no ground why these particular firsts should be distinguished

---

[1] This will be made clearer, inf. p. 123.
[2] See further on this point Dr. Lightfoot's new edition, and the note at the end of this paper.

from others in the Lycian Kalendar, an ordinary one much on the Roman model; but the distinction is full of meaning if conjectured to have been borrowed or transposed from the Asian Kalendar where it is just in these months of thirty-one days, with their double firsts, that a distinctive mark for the true first is of use. Σεβαστή, it may thus be supposed, was in Asia a title of the first or Emperor's birthday [1], specially employed in those months where his birthday needed to be distinguished from its successor, another nominal first.

Still, although February 21st, the former of the two firsts of Xanthicus, might in this way be correctly denominated a' σεβαστή, this does not prove that February 22nd can be β' σεβαστή as required. Can a clue to this further perplexity reside in the coincidence that both A. D. 104 of the Ephesian inscription and A. D. 156, the hypothetical martyrdom, were leap-years?

The leap-year system is of course the characteristic of the Julian Kalendar, which like our own intercalated a day to every fourth February, not however by adding one after the 28th, but by repeating the 24th or 6th before the Kalends, whence the name bissextile. As the Asiatic Kalendar bore a fixed relation to the Julian, it too must have incorporated the intercalated day. But how?

(*a*) Not in the Asiatic February or Dystrus at all. For that ended with its 28th on Feb. 20, and an intercalated or additional day would prevent Xanthicus from beginning on the ninth before the Kalends (Feb. 21) and destroy the whole schematism.

Therefore in Xanthicus [2], which is already of thirty-one days, and must be produced to thirty-two; but

(*b*) Not at the end of Xanthicus, for to end with the

---

[1] Dr. Lightfoot now accepts this view of Usener's, which is supported by a new Pergamene inscription. See inf. p. 152.

[2] *For the discussion of a contrary theory of Archbishop Ussher that the leap-year day was intercalated in September, which has only come under my notice since the body of this paper was in type, see the Appendix, pp. 131 sqq.*

30th is a principle of the kalendar. Therefore just as the 31st day was incorporated at the beginning of the month, so on some similar method must the 32nd have been. Would not the repetition of the 2nd be the natural method?

For there are two conditions which the intercalation of the extra day must satisfy.

> (1) It must be done on the existing principles of the Kalendar; and these clearly suggest the double 2nd.
>
> (2) It must interfere as little as possible with the normal relation of the Asiatic to the Roman Kalendar. But the Julian extra day comes in on the 24th, our hypothetical Asiatic day on the 22nd. Only then on three days of leap-year, Feb. 22, 23, 24, if we are right, will the Julian equivalent of the Asiatic day differ from that of an ordinary year.

These results will be made clearer by a table.

| | *Normal Asiatic Kalendar.* | | | *Conjectural Kalendar for Leap Year.* | | | |
|---|---|---|---|---|---|---|---|
| Feb. 20 | [Dystrus] | | a. d. x Kal. Mart. | a. d. x Kal. Mart. | [Dystrus] | | Feb. 20 |
| 21 | Xanthicus A ΣEB | | ix | ix | Xanthicus A ΣEB | | 21 |
| 22 | | A | viii | viii | | B ΣEB⁹ | 22 |
| 23 | | B | vii | vii | | A | 23 |
| | | | | vi | | B | 24 |
| 24 | | Γ | vi | vi | | Γ | 25 |
| 25 | | Δ | v | v | | Δ | 26 |
| 26 | | E | iv | iv | | E | 27 |
| 27 | | ϛ | iii | iii | | ϛ | 28 |
| 28 | | Z | prid. Kal. Mart. | prid. Kal. Mart. | | Z | 29 |
| Mar. 1 | | H | Kal. Mart. | Kal. Mart. | | H | Mar. 1 |

If the conjecture hazarded as to the meaning of a′ σεβαστή as distinct from a′ be correct, it would follow that β′ σεβαστή of the Ephesian inscription as distinct from β′ meant the earlier as opposed to the latter 2nd. Certainly this 2nd had not the same connection with the Emperor as a′ σεβαστή; but the transference in any case is easy and natural, and the festival which the martyrdom shows to have been proceeding, was apparently (since the Asiarch was president of the games) connected with the κοινὸν 'Ασίας, or Commune Asiae, and therefore with the worship of the Emperors. But the κοινὸν 'Ασίας was arranged on a pentaeteric principle[1], that is, in periods of four years, and it becomes not impossible that one of its celebrations recurred at each leap-year.

The proposed day, Saturday, Feb. 22, the 'high sabbath' of Purim of the year A.D. 156, satisfies thus:—(i) the Proconsul, (ii) the Asiarch, (iii) the Asiatic day and month, (iv) the day of the week, (v) the festival.

It remains only to consider certain subsidiary points on which evidence might be produced in objection to, or in confirmation of, the result attained.

I. The first objection which suggests itself is the equation of the Asiatic date in the Martyrium by the Roman πρὸ ἑπτὰ καλανδῶν Μαρτίων, the 23rd, not the 22nd February. But three alternatives are possible in answer, each of which will rob it of its force. If this equation is due to the original writers, we shall find, if we put ourselves in their position, that some Christian probably possessed a table which equated Asiatic and Julian days like the Hemerology of the MSS., but which, like that, omitted to treat separately of leap-years, and consequently gave the 'seventh before the Kalends of March' as the only equivalent of the 2nd Xanthicus. Or again the original writers may not have written ἑπτὰ at all, but ὀκτώ, which some copyist, who found that in his Hemerology the seventh and not the eighth before the Kalends was the true equivalent, altered into ἑπτά, under the idea that he was benefiting historical accuracy. Or yet, thirdly, the Roman equivalent may not have been given in the original at all, but have been added when the document was being circulated outside Asia, in countries where the Asiatic Kalendar would be unfamiliar and a Roman date would be requisite; the leap-year would of course under these circumstances be forgotten, and the equivalent of the Hemerologies inserted.

II. But in the Acts of Pionius, belonging to A.D. 250 in

---

[1] Cf. on points connected with the Asiarchate the appendix in Lightfoot, ii. pp. 987–998.

the Decian persecution, we are told that the martyr was apprehended 'on the birthday of the blessed martyr Polycarp' on the second day of the sixth month, for which again the Latin gives February 23. Since, however, in Smyrna, reckoning would primarily be kept by the Asiatic Kalendar rather than by the Roman, St. Polycarp's festival would be observed on the 2nd Xanthicus, on whatever Roman day that fell. And as in every year, except leap-year, Xanthicus 2 is really Feb. 23, and A.D. 250 was not leap-year, Feb. 23 was the correct date for the festival in that year.

III. The same explanation is valid if in the old martyrologies, especially in that of the great Syriac MS. of the British Museum (written A.D. 411), Shebat 23—i. e. February 23— is given as St. Polycarp's day; for the ordinary equivalent, and as soon as it was forgotten that the saint suffered in leap-year, the certain equivalent, of Xanthicus 2 was February 23.

IV. More serious is the next, and last, objection which occurs to the writer. In the already mentioned Acts of Pionius the day of that martyr's apprehension is not only the 2nd of Xanthicus, and birthday of St. Polycarp, but also a 'high sabbath.' Now, if this is to have the same meaning for Pionius as for Polycarp, it ought similarly to be tested in relation to Purim and the month of Adar. But in A.D. 250, which is all but certainly the year of those Acts, Nisan 15 fell somewhere about April 4, and Adar 15 consequently about March 6. Here again, just as in the case of Dr. Lightfoot's view in A.D. 155, it would seem that Saturday, Feb. 23, cannot be the preceding or 'high sabbath.'

But is it really probable that in the middle of the third century any Christian writer would intentionally calculate his dates by a Jewish feast? What was natural enough a century earlier, when the Church kept perhaps only two great festivals, and these at least in Asia Minor exactly synchronous with the Passover and Pentecost of the Jews— so that when the Jews calculated their Pascha wrongly, the

Christians did the same—was at this date no longer likely. The Jewish Kalendar would cease to be familiar after the second phase of the great Easter question had begun to agitate the Church, and it was realized that the Jews could not be trusted to fix the true astronomical date for the full moon of Nisan. This conviction was the *raison d'être* of the attempts of Christian scientists to calculate Easter cycles for themselves; and it seems to have been universally acted on by A.D. 250. The 'Paschal Chronicle' of Hippolytus was drawn up as early as A.D. 222, and for half a century this computation or modifications of it apparently held the field, and very probably extended to Asia[1]. But whether this one or another, some Christian system, and no longer the Jewish, must surely by this time have prevailed in Smyrna.

If then it is thus improbable that the Pionian Acts should have reckoned time by the Jewish Kalendar, what explanation is to be given of the 'high sabbath'? Can it have been a Christian festival? Certainly the Eastern Churches kept the Sabbath as a feast, and possibly a sabbath coinciding with the 'birthday' of Polycarp, the patron saint so to speak of the Church of Smyrna, might be treated as a 'high

[1] It is true that the Asiatics were originally Quartodecimans, though they were so no longer at the time of the Council of Nicaea, and perhaps considerably earlier. But in any case they were not Ebionite or Judaizingly inclined Quartodecimans, and there was no reason why they should be less averse to abandoning Jewish errors than other people. Any non-Quartodeciman cycle is serviceable even to Quartodecimans; for as the day of the month (the full moon) had to be fixed before the day of the week (the Sunday after the full moon), all that a Quartodeciman had to do was to utilize the first and neglect the second part of the calculation. Thus Hippolytus formed a 112-years' cycle, after which Easter was to begin to fall again on the same series of days; but astronomically this was only a sixteen years' cycle, after which the full moon was to fall again on the same series of days of the (solar) month, and it was only because the same day of the month would, after an interval of sixteen years, fall on a different day of the week—and so on through the seven days of the week—that the sixteen-years' cycle required to be multiplied by seven before a cycle was attained in which not only the full moon but the Sunday after it fell recurringly on the same series of days of the month.

The wide circulation and adoption in the East of the cycle of Hippolytus (who wrote in Greek) would partly explain the extraordinary vitality of his fame there as compared with the West.

sabbath,' like a red letter Saint's Day coinciding with a Sunday. But a much simpler explanation is permissible. It has apparently escaped even Dr. Lightfoot's notice (at least he lays no stress on it) that the chronological data of the beginning and end of the Pionian Acts, the apprehension and the martyrdom of Pionius, are both modelled on the notice in our Martyrium, as is on comparison abundantly clear [1].

| Acta Pionii, § 2. | Martyrium Polycarpi, § 21. | Acta Pionii, § 23. |
|---|---|---|
| μηνὸς ἕκτου δευτέρᾳ ἱσταμένου [vel ἐνισταμένου] | μηνὸς Ξανθικοῦ δευτέρᾳ ἱσταμένου πρὸ [ἑπτὰ] καλανδῶν Μαρτίων | πρὸ τεσσάρων Ἰδῶν Μαρτίων κατὰ Ῥωμαίους, κατὰ δὲ Ἀσιανοὺς μηνὸς ἕκτου ἐννεακαιδεκάτῃ |
| σαββάτῳ μεγάλῳ [MS. σαββάτου μεγάλου] [2] ... συνελήφθησαν ... | σαββάτῳ μεγάλῳ ὥρᾳ ὀγδόῃ· συνελήφθη ... | ἡμέρᾳ ϲαββάτῳ ὥρᾳ δεκάτῃ |
|  | βασιλεύοντος δὲ εἰς τοὺς αἰῶνας Ἰησοῦ Χριστοῦ, ᾧ ἡ δόξα ...... .... | κατὰ δὲ ἡμᾶς βασιλεύοντος τοῦ Κυρίου ἡμῶν Ἰησοῦ Χριστοῦ, ᾧ ἡ δόξα εἰς τοὺς αἰῶνας τῶν αἰώνων. |
|  | ἀμήν. | ἀμήν. |

| | Martyrium Polycarpi, § 18. | |
|---|---|---|
| ἐν τῇ γενεθλίῳ ἡμέρᾳ τοῦ μακαρίου μάρτυρος Πολυκάρπου. | τὴν τοῦ μαρτυρίου αὐτοῦ ἡμέραν γενέθλιον. | |

Now it becomes explicable that in all the recensions of the Pionian Acts, the final date, that of St. Pionius' martyrdom, is

[1] It may be mentioned in confirmation of this view that the Acts of Pionius are the only instance among some twenty parallels in the Acta Martyrum referred to by Dr. Lightfoot for the 'regnante Jesu Christo,' in which the hour of martyrdom is given.

[2] Either the original writer or a later scribe was ignorant of the meaning of ἱσταμένου in connection with the day of the month, and therefore altered the text so as to construct it with σαββάτου.

said to be a sabbath, whereas in fact it was obviously a Tuesday. But if the 'sabbath' at the end of the Acts was thus an erroneous and parrot-like repetition from the Martyrium of Polycarp, it is not difficult to believe that the 'high sabbath' of the beginning of the Acts may have had the same origin, and the same absence of justification. The apprehension of Pionius coincided alike in the day of the week and of the month with the martyrdom of Polycarp, and if the writers were ignorant, as it is natural to suspect, what the 'high sabbath' really meant in Polycarp's case, they might thoughtlessly assume it to be equally valid with the rest of the data for their own purpose.

Finally there are two arguments to be stated in confirmation of the date proposed in this paper, which seem to make A.D. 156 more probable for the martyrdom than A.D. 155.

I. L. Statius Quadratus was Consul Ordinarius in A.D. 142, and proconsul, on Dr. Lightfoot's view, from A.D. 154 to 155, on that here put forward from A.D. 155 to 156. But (though the data are too few to generalize from with confidence) there is no other instance quoted in the second century where it can be said with certainty that a less interval than thirteen years intervened between consulship and proconsulship[1]; and the extra year allowed here in Quadratus' case is so far a gain.

II. Of more importance is Irenaeus' express statement, made more than once, that Polycarp visited Bishop Anicetus at Rome. But Eusebius, as has been seen, places the accession of Anicetus as late as A.D. 157, and this has to be thrust back two years to allow of a visit from Polycarp in A.D. 155 (probably in summer), even if the martyrdom is placed in A.D. 156; while if the martyrdom is put a year earlier, a three years' transposition of Eusebius' date becomes necessary. It is the serious matter of this extra year which has induced the author of the 'Chronology of the Roman Bishops,' Prof.

[1] See the list in Lightfoot, i. 640; I am assuming that it is exhaustive.

Lipsius, to adopt A.D. 156 in preference to A.D. 155[1]. But then, in order to do so, since Feb. 23 was no sabbath in A.D. 156, he has arbitrarily condemned as spurious the mention of the 'high sabbath,' both in the chronological postscript and in the body of the Martyrium. If the present enquiry has achieved nothing else (and it does not pretend to have done more than to have brought forward another claimant for the true date of the martyrdom), it can at least claim to have based Lipsius' conclusion on intelligible and consistent premisses. Should any other explanation of the 'high sabbath' be put forward, the main objection to A.D. 155 will of course disappear. But so long as the identification with Purim is maintained, so long will it seem that A.D. 156 is a more probable date, and that a hypothesis which makes it a possible year from the point of view of the rest of the evidence is not destitute of support. Such as it is, it is left to the consideration and criticism of students of ecclesiastical history.

[1] But see inf. p. 154.

## Appendix I.

### ON A PASCHAL HOMILY PRINTED IN ST. CHRYSOSTOM'S WORKS ASCRIBED BY USSHER TO A.D. 672. BUT REALLY BELONGING TO A.D. 387.

[C. H. T.]

It was an integral feature of the theory put forward above that the intercalation of the additional day in leap-year took place in Asia almost, though not quite, at the same date as in Rome. But since the preceding Essay was in type the writer has come across an alternative view of the Asiatic intercalation, to which it would be only fair in any case that he should direct attention; but he hopes to be able to show that the fresh evidence thus adduced is really in complete harmony with what was said on pp. 122 sqq.

To Archbishop Ussher, the critic whose sagacity foretold the recovery of the genuine Ignatius, we owe also the first attempt to treat systematically of the Asiatic chronological system, and in particular to take into consideration the leap-year variations[1]. It was indeed a task which without the aid of the Hemerology (and the Hemerology was not known before A.D. 1715) would probably have never met with complete success, for the intercalation of the repeated first was an expedient not likely to have suggested itself even to the acutest scholar. But unfortunately Ussher had also not perceived that the Macedonian kalendars of Syria and of Asia, though they used the same twelve names for the months, did not use them of the same months, each month in Syria having the name of the month next preceding in Asia. Thus while in Asia Xanthicus (as the Hemerology tells us) was equivalent to late February and March, in Syria it was practically equivalent to April. Of these two reckonings the Syrian was by far the commoner, and Ussher assumed it to be the only one; so that when St Polycarp suffered on the 2nd Xanthicus, this ought to fall (not in February but) at the end of March or beginning of April. Now the Paschal Chronicle actually does place the martyrdom, not with the text of the Martyrium on a. d. vii Kal. Mart.,

---

[1] *De Macedonum et Asianorum Anno Solari*, reprinted in vol. ix. of Gronovius, *Thesaurus Graecarum Antiquitatum*, pp. 1205–1268.

*printed in the Works of St. Chrysostom* 131

but a month later, on a. d. vii Kal. Apr. (March 26)¹; and Ussher following its authority, concluded that Xanthicus, the seventh month of the kalendar, commenced on March 25.

Now in a Paschal Homily attributed by Balsamon to St. Chrysostom, and printed in Savile's edition of that father (vol. v. pp. 940-949) from a MS. belonging to Gabriel, Archbishop of Philadelphia, the author is apparently addressing his congregation just before Lent began, on the subject of the date of Easter, which was falling that year later (so it was said) than had ever been known before— later certainly than the heretics or the Jews were keeping it on that occasion ²—' on the second day of the eighth month.' April 25 is the latest day on which Easter according to any reckoning was ever made to fall; hence the eighth month cannot begin later than April 24. But the Homilist also speaks of the '26th day of the seventh month' as falling exactly a week earlier (than the 2nd of the eighth month), that is, not later than April 18; from which Ussher saw that it followed that the seventh month itself cannot begin, as from the day of St. Polycarp he had deduced that it ought to begin, on March 25, but at latest March 24. Consequently he supposed that this difference of a day must be due to leap-year, the intercalation being made at Rome in February, in Asia as he conjectured at the end of the Asiatic year in September, so that all Asiatic dates between February and September will, if transposed into Roman reckoning, appear a day earlier than usual. If the Paschal Homily falls in leap-year, its seventh month would then begin correctly on March 24, and not, as in other years, on March 25. Since then in only one instance between A.D. 140 and A.D. 919—in A.D. 672—did Easter fall simultaneously on April 25 and in leap-year, Ussher concludes that this is the only admissible date for the Homily in question.

That Ussher was building on a radically unsound foundation when he supposed that St. Polycarp's death and the 2nd of Xanthicus had anything to do with March 26 we now know; and we also know from the Hemerology that in fact the seventh Asiatic month

---

¹ No doubt because like Ussher the chronicler writing after 600 A.D., was ignorant of any but the Syrian nomenclature for the months. In Asia the names had dropped out, and had been succeeded by numbers ('first month,' etc.), comparatively early; cf. Lightfoot, i. 677, 678. Numbers are used in the Acts of Pionius and by the Paschal Homily discussed below; but the (Asiatic) month Apellaeus occurs in Epiphanius, *Haer.* 51. § 24; see inf., p. 149.

² P. 940. 18: αἱρετικοὶ ἀποσκιρτήσαντες φαίνονται καὶ Ἰουδαῖοι ἐπαγγέλλονται πάσχα τελεῖν.

K 2

(Artemisius) began on March 24, exactly in accordance with the Paschal Homily. Cardinal Noris, writing on the same subject as Ussher, but like him before the publication of the Hemerology, was unable to make the latter correction, but (following Valesius) he rightly pointed out the distinction between the Syriac and the Asiatic Xanthicus, and restored St. Polycarp to February. At the same time, curiously enough, he accepts unreservedly Ussher's conclusions on the Paschal Homily, apparently oblivious that they too rested in the end entirely on the false Polycarpian basis.

The Paschal Homily ceases therefore to bear witness against us. But why may not it be put into the box in our own favour? It is so interesting in itself, and because its date can be fixed with such precision, that we propose to enter at some length into this byway of history, and to preface the enquiry by summarizing the contents of the Homily, which aims at supporting the scientific accuracy of the late Easter by a thoroughgoing exposition of the principles on which the Church calculations were based.

In the first place some were accustomed to ask why when Christmas and Epiphany[1] as well as the commemorations of the martyrs were fixed feasts, Easter alone should be moveable? The answer is, that in the case of Easter three conditions have to be combined; the month must be the first month—that is, the first after the spring equinox; the moon must be not less than at the full—that is the fourteenth; and three days of the week, Friday, Saturday, Sunday, have to be taken into account. Even the Jews combined what they believed to be the first month with the fourteenth day of the moon for their Passover; and they are followed by the Quartodeciman[2] heresy and—so far—by the

---

[1] Christmas on the 8th before the Kalends of January according to the Romans, i.e. Dec. 25; Epiphany on the 13th of the fourth month according to the Asians, i.e. according to the Asiatic Kalendar, as explained above, Jan. 6. See further below.

[2] For the Quartodecimans and Novatians cf. Sozomen, vii. 18 (p. 739, Hussey): πλὴν τούτων [certain Novatians] καὶ τῶν ἐπὶ τῆς Ἀσίας καλουμένων τεσσαρεσκαιδεκατιτῶν ὁμοίως Ῥωμαίοις καὶ Αἰγυπτίοις καὶ οἱ ἀπὸ τῶν ἄλλων αἱρέσεων ταύτην τὴν ἑορτὴν ἄγουσιν· ἀλλ' οἱ μὲν ἐν αὐτῇ τῇ τεσσαρεσκαιδεκαταίᾳ σὺν τοῖς Ἰουδαίοις ἑορτάζουσιν, ὅθεν ὧδε ὀνομάζονται· οἱ δὲ Ναυατιανοὶ τὴν ἀναστάσιμον ἡμέραν ἐπιτελοῦσιν· Ἰουδαίοις δὲ καὶ αὐτοὶ ἕπονται καὶ εἰς ταὐτὸ τοῖς τεσσαρεσκαιδεκατίταις καταστρέφουσι· πλὴν εἰ μὴ τύχοι τῇ ιδ' τῆς σελήνης ἡ πρώτη τοῦ σαββάτου ἡμέρα συμπεσοῦσα, κατόπιν γίνονται τῶν Ἰουδαίων ὅσαις ἂν ἡμέραις συμβαίη τὴν ἐρχομένην κυριακὴν ὑστερίζειν τῆς τεσσαρεσκαιδεκαταίας τῆς σελήνης.

## printed in the Works of St. Chrysostom. 133

Novatians. The Montanists indeed reckon the fourteenth not by the lunar but by the solar month, and always take the fourteenth of the seventh (solar) Asiatic month[1]; but this obviously contra-

That is, Quartodecimans kept exactly to the Jewish fourteenth, on whatever day of the week it fell. The Novatians in question, on the other hand, always observed Friday and Sunday—as the Paschal Homilist puts it, ἐπὶ τὴν τριήμερον ἔρχονται—but (1) accepted the Jewish reckoning for the ιδ'; (2) even assuming that to be correct, they made another fault, for if it fell on Sunday, they kept that as Easter Day. This does not apply to all Novatians, but to those of Galatia and Phrygia, who decided to 'Judaize' with regard to Easter at the Council of Pazus (Παζουκώμη in Phrygia) under Valens, i. e. circa 370 A.D. Those of Rome celebrated with the Catholic Church; and Socrates says the same of those of Constantinople and Nicomedia; cf. his parallel account, H. E. iv. 28, v. 21. A Bithynian synod of Novatians allowed either method (Soc. v. 21; Soz. vii. 18).

[1] That is, according to the Kalendar (p. 113, sup.), April 6.

Sozomen (vii. 18, quoted by Ussher) gives us similar but fuller information about the Montanist Easter. According to him, they commenced their year with the spring equinox, the beginning of creation, because the two lights, sun and moon, by which times and years are regulated, came then into being. At the end of every eight years the cycles of sun and moon will fall together at this time, eight years of the sun being equivalent to 99 lunations. Their first date they fixed on March 24, and interpreting the scriptural fourteenth of the month then begun, it would fall on a. d. viii. Id. Apr. i. e. April 6, Easter being kept on the Sunday after this day, i. e. from the 7th to the 13th of April: for Scripture says 'from the 14th to the 21st.'

(1) Ussher, by interpolating conjecturally the words εἰ δὲ μή, interprets the last words to mean that if the 14th (April 6) coincided with the Sunday, that and not the next Sunday was the Montanist Easter.

(2) Ussher also asserts Sozomen to be in error in fixing the 'fourteenth of the first month' on April 6 instead of April 7. It was part of his whole theory that March 25 was the first of the month, and he supposes the mention of March 24 in this passage to be a copyist's alteration, to suit the (erroneous) April 6 as the 14th; especially as the Latin Tripartite History reads a. d. viii, not a. d. ix, Kal. Apr. But we know now from the Hemerology (which was unknown to Ussher) that the Asiatic, Ephesian, and Bithynian month did begin on March 24, and that in consequence Sozomen's April 6 and the Homilist's 14th of the Asiatic seventh month are in perfect harmony. It is not the Greek of Sozomen, but the Latin of the Tripartite History which has suffered corruption, doubtless owing to the importance of the date March 25 in the West.

It would be unprofitable to attempt to explain the origin of the error of the Montanist computation. The sect was not a cultured one, and in despair it cut, instead of attempting to untie, the Gordian knot. One thing however is tolerably clear, that March 24 was taken as the starting-point of their first month because it began a month in the 'Asiatic' Kalendar.

It has been pointed out to me that Duchesne (*Origines du Culte Chrétien*, p. 251) comparing Hippolytus' date for the Passion, March 25, with the Western Christmas, Dec. 25, and this Montanist date for the Passion, April 6,

dicts the record of the Passion of Christ on the fourteenth of the moon at the Jewish Passover. However, they too observed the τριήμερος, the Friday, Saturday, and Sunday.

The error of the Jews was that they were not really careful to fix their first month by the equinox. The wise men of the Jews—Philo, Josephus, and others[1]—had stated the true method, and some of them lived even after the time of Christ, so that doubtless Christ suffered at a Passover correctly reckoned; and, as a matter of fact, the Acts of Pilate relate that the crucifixion took place on the eighth before the Kalends of April (March 25)[2]. But after the Jews had rejected Christ, they took to rejecting also all their own ancient guides. The two and seventy[3] approved translators of the Scriptures were thrown over in favour of a single proselyte[4].

with the Eastern Christmas, Jan. 6, supposes that the two dates for the Passion suggested the two dates for Christmas. I should have thought the converse more likely in the Eastern case.

[1] On this anti-Jewish equinoctial controversy see Anatolius, Socrates, and the Apostolic Constitutions quoted above, p. 119. Anatolius (ap. Eus. *H. E.* vii. 32) names Philo, Josephus, Musaeus, and those 'even more ancient,' the two Agathobuli and Aristobulus. Sozomen (vii. 18), referring to Anatolius as 'Eusebius,' names Philo, Josephus, and Aristobulus.

[2] Similarly Epiphanius (*Haer.* 50. 1), who tells us that certain Quartodecimans did always observe March 25, τῇ πρὸ ὀκτὼ καλανδῶν Ἀπριλλίων, as the day of Christ's death, on the strength of the same *Acta Pilati*. He adds that he had himself found copies of the *Acta* which contained the 18th of March, πρὸ δεκάπεντε καλανδῶν Ἀπριλλίων. The year of the Passion was originally given in the *Acta* as the 15th of Tiberius (A.D. 28-29) in accordance with the earliest Christian tradition (for I feel no doubt, in spite of the arguments of Lipsius' *Pilatus-Acten*, that the alternative dates, 18th or 19th Tiberius, are alterations due to the influence of the *Chronicle* of Eusebius, who set the fashion for subsequent writers), and it is an extraordinarily striking coincidence that if the Crucifixion did take place in the year A. D. 29, the day must beyond question have been March 18, as pointed out in Browne's *Ordo Saeclorum*. Meanwhile the 18th of March was altered to that day week, March 25, probably under the influence of the Chronicle of Hippolytus, in which this was the day given for the Passion, and also because March 18 would soon be looked on as an inadmissible day, through its falling before the equinox.

[3] 72 is given by the Letter of Aristeas, by Tertullian (*Apol.* 18), and by Epiphanius (*de Pond. et Mens.* iii-vi); 70 by Irenaeus (iii. 21), by Anatolius (Eus. *H. E.* vii. 32), by Jerome, and by Augustine.

[4] That is, Aquila. Irenaeus indeed (iii. 21) calls both Theodotion and Aquila proselytes, but there can be no doubt which is meant here, for it was Aquila's translation which because of its superior literalness came into favour with the Jews, while Christian writers believed that Aquila and the Jews who followed him were animated by anti-Christian bias in their attempt to supersede a translation which favoured, and was favoured by, the Christian Church.

## printed in the Works of St. Chrysostom. 135

The equinoctial rule, though a tradition of Moses himself, was neglected, and now the Jewish Passover fell indifferently before or after, but on the present occasion (εἰς τὸ ἐνεστώς) before, the equinox.

Now what was the mystical fitness of the date at which Christ suffered ?

That the equinox should mark the commencement of the first month is clear, if we think of the original creation of the world, for the first day and night would naturally have been equal : and it must have been the spring equinox, for the creation of flowers and trees and plants, symbols of spring, immediately followed. And so Scripture says that God divided equally the light and the darkness ; ἀνὰ μέσον τοῦ φωτὸς καὶ ἀνὰ μέσον τοῦ σκότους. Then after the equinox on the fourth day, God created the sun and the moon—at the full; on the sixth day, man; on the seventh He rested; and on the eighth, which is the first again, He suffered the now perfect universe to start on its course. So when man, created though he was in the image of God, had fallen from his high estate, and the Only-begotten Son had come to earth to restore him, He employs for redemption the same portion and period of time He had before chosen and used for creation, that the end might be harmonious with the beginning. Consequently the week of the Passion—the fulness of the times, the recapitulation of all things—must combine, just as the week of creation had done, the equinox, the full moon, and the sixth day or Friday specially devoted to man. But a week whose commencement on Sunday coincides with the equinox and contains the full moon, is an infrequent occurrence; we read therefore in the Gospels that though the Jews had long sought Him, He had evaded them, until 'His hour was come,' and then He willingly suffered. After the equinox, when the light began to gain ground on and to master the darkness, but not later than the first Friday after, on which too He had created man, He suffered ; and on the Sabbath again, after the completion of His work, He rested.

But all these different data obviously cannot converge every year. They were necessarily observed in the one great Pascha, but just as that one sacrifice needs no repetition but only an imitation (μίμημα) in the Eucharist, so in our Pascha we need only imitate the season as far as lies in our power, combining the equinox, the fourteenth of the moon, and the three days' celebration. Avoiding the ignorance of Jews and heretics, we find the equinox, we look for the next full moon, and so for the Preparation, Sabbath and Lord's Day[1].

Further, the Lord fulfilled exactly the law of Moses, that on the fourteenth day between the evenings the lamb should be slaughtered: for 'between the evenings' will be at the ninth hour, as learned Jews fix it, and at the ninth hour Jesus, the Lamb of God, gave up the ghost[2]. Again, the darkness at the crucifixion was not without its special meaning. To the Jews it recalled the prophecies of Zechariah and Amos, that it should be neither day nor night, and at eventide it should be light; that the sun should go down at midday; if the prophet added that their feasts should be turned to grief, this was actually the case, we learn from history, at the siege of Jerusalem[3]. By the Gentiles, the miracle of the darkness could not be explained away with Greek artifice as an eclipse, for the moon at the Passover is at the full: and by celebrating the Pascha yearly at full moon, we have a yearly reminder of the miracle for all ages and all men[4].

---

[1] Cf. Epiphanius, *Haer.* 50. 3: διὸ παρατηρούμεθα μὲν τὴν τεσσαρεσκαιδεκάτην, ὑπερβαίνομεν δὲ τὴν ἰσημερίαν, φέρομεν δὲ ἐπὶ τὴν ἁγίαν κυριακὴν τὸ τέλος τῆς συμπληρώσεως.

[2] Therefore the Homilist follows the 'Johannine' view that our Lord ate only an anticipatory Passover and suffered on the 14th Nisan. This is in accordance with the almost unanimous view of early writers (Apollinaris, Clement of Alexandria, Irenaeus, Tertullian, Hippolytus; see Westcott, *Introduction to Gospels*, p. 347), but in disagreement with an equally strong *consensus* later the other way. Even at the earliest possible date for our Homily, St. Chrysostom (a fact quite sufficient to disprove his authorship) and St. Ambrose (see his epistle, inf. p. 147), hold to the fifteenth; similarly Proterius of Alexandria, in his letter to Leo of Rome about the Easter of A. D. 455; and though the Paschal Chronicle, built up seemingly out of earlier materials, witnesses to a survival of the older opinion, yet in the ninth century Photius, impressed as he is with the evidence of two early writers, still speaks of them as varying from 'the Church' (Cod. 115, 116, fin., καὶ σκοπεῖν χρή. ὁ γὰρ Χρυσόστομος καὶ ἡ ἐκκλησία τότε φησὶν αὐτὸν ἐπιτελέσαι τὸ νομικὸν πρὸ τοῦ μυστικοῦ δείπνου).

[3] The Homilist adds, διετῇ χρόνον ὁ πόλεμος κατὰ τοὺς Ἰουδαίους ἐπὶ πένθη ἀνάλωσε, p. 947. 24.

[4] This was the argument of Julius Africanus, early in the 3rd century, (*Chronicon* fragm. ap. Routh, *R. S.* ii. 297), τοῦτο τὸ σκότος ἔκλειψιν τοῦ ἡλίου Θάλλος ἀποκαλεῖ ἐν τρίτῳ τῶν ἱστοριῶν, ὡς ἐμοὶ δοκεῖ ἀλόγως (he explains about the full moon) ... ἦν σκότος θεοποίητον διότι τὸν Κύριον συνέβη παθεῖν. Origen, who had himself explained the darkness as an eclipse (*c. Celsum*, ii. 33), in his Commentary on St. Matthew, adopted Africanus' view; cf. Routh, l. c. p. 479, ἵνα γὰρ μὴ εἴπωσιν ἔκλειψιν εἶναι τὸ γεγεννημένον, διὰ τοῦτο τῇ ιδ΄ γίνεται, ὅτε ἔκλειψιν συμβῆναι ἀμήχανον. But Eusebius (followed by Jerome, and as usual by the later chronologers) still called the darkness an eclipse, identifying

### *printed in the Works of St. Chrysostom.* 137

Now to apply these investigations to the fixing of the current feast. Twelve full moons after the last Easter we naturally expect the next to fall. But if the twelfth falls before the equinox, we must intercalate a thirteenth lunar month in order to get to a full moon after the equinox[1]. Thus, in the present year, the twelfth full moon or fourteenth of the twelfth month falls two days before the equinox, and we must look for the next full moon for our Pascha. We have thus settled two of the conditions, the equinox and the full moon; we have still to find the Sunday. Now the postponed fourteenth will itself fall on a Sunday, and therefore to get our three days, Friday, Saturday, Sunday, we must again defer Easter for a week, or the festival of the resurrection would fall on the 14th, which is the date of the Passion.

Of the two full moons under discussion, the first falls, as we said, two days before the equinox[2]; the second on the 26th day of the seventh month, and Easter exactly a week later on the second day of the eighth month[3].

---

it with one mentioned by the historian Phlegon under A. D. 32, which thenceforward became the usual year to which the crucifixion was assigned (see Lipsius, *Pilatus-Acten*, p. 23 ff.).

[1] Since twelve lunations (at 29½ days each) amount to only about 354 days, there is a defect of rather more than 11 days on the total as compared with the solar year. This defect goes on increasing, and when it would bring a thirteenth full moon before the spring equinox, a thirteenth or intercalary month is added to the old year.

[2] πρὸ δύο ἡμερῶν τῆς ἰσημερίας—'the day before,' I suppose; on the analogy of phrases like τῇ τρίτῃ for ' the day before yesterday' (Field on Matt. xvi. 12 *Otium Norvicense, Pars Tertia*, p. 7) and Latin 'ante diem tertium.'

The cycle of Hippolytus (A. D. 222) had placed the equinox on March 18, and this reckoning prevailed in Rome till the fifth century; but the cycle of Anatolius (A. D. 277) advanced it to March 19, and the Alexandrian modification of the latter cycle, prevalent in the fourth century throughout the East, placed it later still, on March 21 (Hefele, *Councils*, E. T. i. p. 320). Our Homilist argued above that the crucifixion on March 25 corresponded to the Friday or sixth day of Creation week; the division of light and darkness, that is the equinox, would then have taken place on the first day of the same week, March 20. But I doubt whether he really intended to differ from the Alexandrine computation in practice: he would, I believe, have agreed that the 21st March was the first legal day for the ιδ', and the 22nd for Easter Day. In any case the full moon meant must have fallen on March 19 or 20, for the next fell on the 26th day of the seventh month, which on the principles of the Asiatic Kalendar (the month beginning a. d. ix Kal. Apr., i. e. March 24, and being like April a month of 30 days not repeating its first) would be the 18th of April.

[3] The eighth Asiatic month begins a. d. ix Kal. Mai., April 23, and being, like May, of 31 days, it repeats its first; the second will therefore fall on April 25.

If it was argued that Easter never had fallen so late as it was now proposed to hold it, proof against this statement could be brought by witnesses of good memory (μνήμονες μάρτυρες). How often in the past do you suppose it has been said, 'It has never been the case' (οὐδέποτε γέγονε) and yet science prevails? Moreover the objectors admit that Easter has often fallen as late as the 29th day of the seventh month [1], and the difference between us is therefore narrowed down to three or four days, which they shrink from yielding to the claims of science. And if it was simply a matter of prejudice against variations in the date of Easter, why there was variation between every two successive celebrations. In the current and three following years Easter would fall (i) on the 2nd of the eighth month, (ii) then on the 17th of the seventh month, (iii) then on the 9th of the seventh month, (iv) lastly on the 29th of the seventh month [2].

And such variations are all direct consequences of the two rules of the full moon after the equinox and the Sunday after the full moon. As to the latter point, if the full moon or 14th falls in the middle (πλάτος) of the week, the matter is simple, the next Sunday is Easter; but if it falls about the Sunday, then great caution is necessary. For instance, in the present case, careless calculators tried to make out that the fourteenth of the moon fell on the Saturday [i.e. April 17] and that therefore the next day was Easter Sunday [3]. But they were quite mistaken; even impartial and in-

---

[1] That is, April 21. Cp. the preface to the Festal Letters of St. Athanasius (quoted in Hefele, ii. 159), 'the Romans stated that they possessed a tradition, as ancient as the time of St. Peter, that they were not to go beyond the 21st of April:' and cf. the Epistle of St. Ambrose, inf. p. 148. Our Homilist cannot mean that any living witnesses could testify to an Easter on April 25: for according to Ussher (l. c. p. 1228) between A. D. 140 and 919, Easter fell on that day only four times, A. D. 387, 482, 577, 672; and a period of 95 years is more than any memory could embrace. What he undoubtedly does mean is that while the objectors opposed April 25 on the ground that April 21 was the last possible day for Easter, fairly modern instances could be quoted where this limit had been overpassed, i. e. where Easter had been held on April 22, 23, or 24.

[2] That is, by the Asiatic Kalendar, April 25, April 9, April 1, April 21.

[3] Consequently, if the 14th had fallen on Saturday, the next day would have been admitted to be Easter Sunday, even though this made the commemoration of the Passion fall on the 13th. All that was contended for was that the feast of the Sunday should fall clear of the fast of the 14th. This was the principle of the Alexandrine cycle; but Hippolytus and Anatolius (and the Roman Church still in the fourth century) would have put off Easter for a week, even if the Saturday had fallen on the ιδ'.

telligent pagans (σοφοὶ τῶν Ἑλλήνων) could tell them that as a matter of fact the fourteenth coincided with the Sunday and the night after it, almost into the following Monday, and not near the Saturday at all; so that quite obviously Easter must be postponed for another week.

Facts must be faced; disputes must be put aside; the mind must be clear for the right observation of the seven weeks of Lent, the first of which, according to the true calculation of Easter, was now just about to begin[1].

Such is a tolerably ample analysis of the Homily on which Archbishop Ussher's leap-year theory rests, and it is obvious at once that it contains sufficient marks of time—in particular the dates of four successive Easters—to aid us in a secure reconstruction of its kalendar even for leap-year. It is now proposed to treat in order (1) of the locality of the Homily, (2) of the rough date of the Homily, (3) of the kalendar employed and the year which it suggests, (4) of other special evidence pointing to the same date.

(1) The presumption raised by two mentions of Asiatic months only comes in to reinforce a conclusion which could be safely drawn even without it. The seven weeks' Lenten fast excludes—at least on the fifth-century evidence of the historians Socrates and Sozomen—Illyria, Greece, Egypt and Palestine; while it would fall in with any part of the country from Constantinople round to Phoenicia. The mention of certain heretics in connection with erroneous Paschal observances (notes on pp. 132, 133) narrows the field still further. The Quartodecimans are called by Socrates

---

[1] No doubt the Paschal quarrel with which our Homilist is concerned was excited in his Church by a dispute whether Lent should not have begun before.

For these seven weeks of Lent cf. Sozomen, vii. 19 (p. 743, Hussey), οἱ μὲν εἰς ἓξ ἑβδομάδας ἡμερῶν λογίζονται, ὡς Ἰλλύριοι καὶ οἱ πρὸς δύσιν, Λιβύη τε πᾶσα καὶ Αἴγυπτος σὺν τοῖς Παλαιστίνοις· οἱ δὲ ἑπτὰ ὡς ἐν Κωνσταντινουπόλει καὶ τοῖς περὶξ ἔθνεσι μέχρι Φοινίκων· ἄλλοι δὲ τρεῖς σποραδὴν ἐν ταῖς ἓξ ἢ ἑπτὰ νηστεύουσιν· οἱ δὲ ἅμα τρεῖς πρὸ τῆς ἑορτῆς συνάπτουσιν· οἱ δὲ δύο ὡς οἱ τὰ Μοντάνου φρονοῦντες. In the parallel passage of Socrates (H E v 22, p. 240, Bright), I believe the historian's meaning to be that those whom he does not specify fasted for seven weeks, his point being that many people who fasted less than 40 days yet called Lent τεσσαρακοστή, which, strictly speaking, only those who fasted seven weeks continuously had a right to do. He has only therefore to mention the exceptions to this latter rule.

(v. 22), and by Sozomen (vii. 18) οἱ ἐν 'Ασίᾳ, οἱ ἐπὶ τῆς 'Ασίας. The Novatians were powerful in Constantinople, the Hellespont, Phrygia, Paphlagonia and Galatia; but the erroneous Pascha blamed by the Homilist was adopted not by the Novatians of Rome or even those of Constantinople and Nicomedia, but by those of Phrygia and Galatia only. And lastly the Montanists, as we know and as their alternative titles of Πεπουζῖται and Φρύγες (Soz. vii. 18) clearly show, were always a distinctively Phrygian sect. Our Homilist then certainly wrote in Asia Minor, and probably somewhere not far removed from Phrygia.

(2) From evidence of place we pass to evidence of similar sort for time; and here again the various sects and religions with which the Church, according to the Homily, has to deal, will first come under review[1]. Of Montanism as still flourishing in Phrygia we hear in the laws of Constantine, in the council of Laodicea, and in St. Basil in the fourth century, and in the Theodosian code and the historian Sozomen during the first half of the fifth; but in the middle of the sixth century it appears to have been finally exterminated by the persecution of Justinian. Similarly the Novatians of Asia Minor were in the fourth and fifth centuries numerous and influential, as we learn from Epiphanius, Basil, and Socrates; but after the fifth century not much is heard of them. In particular the judaizing Novatians, with whom alone our Homily deals, seem after A.D. 450 to have finally coalesced with Montanism. Judaism is introduced in the Homily mainly in connection with the relation of the equinox to the Passover, a form of dispute especially characteristic of the third and fourth centuries, for it appears in Anatolius of Laodicea, at the Council of Nicaea, in the Apostolic Constitutions and in St. Ambrose. One would not imagine that references to it would be frequent later; and with every century the intercourse even of heretical Christianity with Judaism must have been growing appreciably smaller. Lastly Pagans ("Ελληνες) are even in Asia Minor still a force which must be taken into account. Our Homilist had just been preaching against both Jews and Pagans. The annual memory of the miraculous darkness of the crucifixion is an annual rebuke to Pagan unbelief. And scientific Pagans are quoted as admitting the accuracy of the astronomical calculations of the Church for Easter. All this

---

[1] For the summaries on this and the following pages I am largely indebted to various articles in the Dictionaries of Christian Biography and Antiquities.

*printed in the Works of St. Chrysostom.* 141

is not surprising in the fourth century; it becomes stranger for the fifth, and it would be almost incredible later.

The Gospel chronology again shows an independence of Eusebius, which suggests a date not later than 400 A.D., after which time there were few writers who, like Epiphanius and our Homilist, were uninfluenced by the *Chronicle*. For instance, the crucifixion is placed on Nisan 14 in common with a catena of primitive fathers, but against the view of Ambrose, Chrysostom, Proterius, and the later centuries. The 25th of March is given (after the Acts of Pilate) for the crucifixion with Hippolytus, Tertullian, and Augustine. The darkness of the crucifixion is explained with Africanus and Origen as a miracle, and not with Eusebius, Malala, and the Paschal Chronicle as Phlegon's eclipse.

Finally an argument may be drawn from the fact that Christmas, Epiphany, and the commemorations of martyrs are mentioned as the feasts kept at that time in the Church on fixed days. For the saints' days parallels may be found at least as early as a Gothic fragment of the fourth century, the Syriac Kalendar in the great MS. dated A.D. 411, or the Roman lists traceable to the fourth and fifth centuries [1]. Of the fixed feasts commemorative of the Gospel history, Christmas and Epiphany are also the two mentioned in the Apostolic Constitutions (v. 13), while the Paschal Chronicle, for instance, in the seventh century has the Purification, the Annunciation and the Nativity of St. John Baptist; and of these three the first at least was instituted by the Emperor not later than about A.D. 540.

On the other hand it might perhaps be urged that the commemoration of the Nativity on Dec. 25 rather than on Jan. 6, is for the East an innovation which points to a date later than Chrysostom, who in an Antiochene Homily thought to have been delivered in A.D. 386 speaks of the transference of the festival as introduced from the West less than ten years before. But (i) our Homily is not earlier, as will be seen, than A.D. 387: (ii) the change at Antioch may have taken place later than in other parts of the East; the Apostolic Constitutions give Dec. 25, and they are apparently earlier than Chrysostom: (iii) it is not unreasonable to conjecture that when our Homilist in the same context defines Christmas by a Roman, and Epiphany by an Asiatic date (κατὰ 'Ρωμαίους, κατ' 'Ασιανούς) that the former feast somehow connected itself in his

---

[1] Duchesne, p. 278.

mind with the West, in which case he must have lived before the origin of the December celebration was forgotten. Not even here then have we any evidence tending to suggest a date later than the fourth century for our Homily.

(3) Now if an Asiatic writer use once a Roman method of dating (and this, as we have just seen, perhaps from a special reason) for Christmas-day, but an Asiatic method (κατ' Ἀσιανοὺς) twice, for Epiphany and for the Montanist Easter, we shall conclude that his normal Kalendar was the Asiatic, and shall turn to it for help when we find him giving dates for several successive Easters on what is at any rate not a Roman reckoning; and we shall not be surprised that the characteristic features of the 'Asiatic' Kalendars of the Hemerology are faithfully reproduced in the Homily. The Montanist fourteenth for the Pascha was reckoned on the fourteenth of the seventh Asiatic month; the Hemerology commences the seventh month on a. d. ix Kal. Apr. (March 24), and as a month of 30 days does not repeat its first, and thus its 14th will fall on April 6th, a. d. viii Id. Apr., exactly the Roman date as given by Sozomen in the same connexion. The Epiphany festival of the Church was on the 13th of the fourth Asiatic month, which beginning on a. d. ix Kal. Jan. (Dec. 24), and as a month of 31 days repeating its first, brings us to January 6, the well-known festival of the Eastern Church[1], as

[1] Jan. 6 for the Epiphany, e. g. in Apost. Const. v. 13, ἡ ἐπιφάνιος . . . γινέσθω . . . ἕκτῃ τοῦ δεκάτου μηνός; in the Kalendarium Karthaginense (Ruinart, Acta Sincera, p. 634), viii Idus Jan. sanctum Epefania. It is true that we do find allusions to Jan. 5, instead of Jan. 6, and it might therefore be argued that this is possibly the day intended here, the Asiatics having by this time dropped the repetition of the first day in months of 31 days. But such allusions all belong to times or places where in accordance with the earliest custom the Epiphany was celebrated in conjunction with the feast of the Nativity; and the latter was commemorated at night; cf. the 'Constitutions of the Alexandrian Church' (Dict. Chr. Ant. i. p. 359), 'in die autem Nativitatis et Epiphaniae . . . ut noctu missa celebretur'; and so Cosmas Indicopleustes (c. A.D. 550) can even say that all Christians concur in celebrating the Nativity on (Choeac 28 =) Dec. 24. Similarly Stephen Gobar (Photius, cod. 232) in his list of disputed questions names the two dates for the Nativity, one of which is Ἰανουαρίῳ ἓ κατὰ τὸ μέσον τῆς νυκτὸς ἥτις ἐστὶ πρὸ ὀκτὼ εἰδῶν Ἰανουαρίων, i. e. Jan. 5 and 6. Thus so far as Epiphanius (Haer. 51. 24) speaks of the 5th of January, it is to be noticed (i) that he is speaking of the Nativity only; the Baptism he placed on Nov. 8; (ii) that he explains the date πέμπτῃ Ἰανουαρίου ἑσπέρα εἰς ἕκτην ἐπιφώσκουσα, and as πρὸ ὀκτὼ εἰδῶν = Jan. 6; (iii) that the Egyptian, Greek, Paphian, and Arabic equivalents given in the same passage are shown by the Hemerology to apply only to Jan. 6. And similarly the Armenian Church, combining in one the

*printed in the Works of St. Chrysostom.* 143

its 14th. Thirdly, the Paschal full moon of the year in which the Homily was delivered fell on the 26th day of the seventh month, while the second day of the eighth month was exactly a week later. But the seventh Asiatic month commenced on a. d. ix Kal. Apr. (March 24), and the eighth on a. d. ix Kal. Mai. (April 23); the 26th day of the seventh month (one of 30 days only) falls on April 18, and therefore that day week is April 25. But if the eighth month began on April 23, and the 2nd of it fell on the 25th, the repetition of the first in months of 31 days must still have formed an integral part of the Asiatic system.

Now however the possibility must be taken into account that the year of the Homily was a leap-year, and the intercalation of the extra day was not made in Asia till at any rate after April. If this were so, as each Asiatic day would be equivalent to one (Roman) day earlier than usual, the two dates of the Homily would become April 17 and April 24. We should then have to find a year in which, on the Alexandrine cycle, the following conditions were satisfied:—($a$) full moon on April 17; ($b$) Easter a week later on April 24; ($c$) the year *ex hypothesi* a leap-year.

Taking as our guide the Paschal table of Dionysius Exiguus (Migne, *Patrologia Latina*, vol. 67, p. 493), who first introduced Alexandrian calculations in a scientific form to the West, we have there given full moons and Easters from A.D. 513 to 626, those from A.D. 532 to 626 forming a complete set of 95 years[1]. Now the selection of 95 years as the cycle was prompted by the desire to find a term of years after which (1) 95 being a multiple of 19, and

commemoration of the Annunciation, Nativity, and Epiphany, commenced with the Annunciation on the evening of Jan. 5, and so apparently proceeded to the Nativity and Epiphany (D. Chr. Ant. *ut sup.*). But our Homilist, unlike this, distinguished between the Nativity on Dec. 25, and the Epiphany on Jan. 6.

It is true that St. Jerome explains the date of the prophecy of Ezekiel i. 'in the thirteenth year, in the fourth month, on the fifth day of the month,' as foreshadowing Christ's Baptism in His thirtieth year, on the fifth day of the fourth (Eastern) month. But this is a forced application of a prophecy; and moreover St. Jerome was writing in Palestine, where the joint celebration of the two feasts had not yet been superseded (Duchesne, p 248), so that the 5th would still form part of the feast. In fact his strong disclaimer, at this very point, of the union of the two, almost suggests that he is borrowing his interpretation from some previous writer who had interpreted the prophetic date of both Nativity and Epiphany. (See his Commentary *in loc.* quoted by Ussher, p. 1216.)

[1] No doubt there exists a list of all occasions on which Easter has been held; and if I had known where to find it, I might have spared myself the calculations from this point for a page onwards.

the Alexandrine lunar cycle being of 19 years, the full moons would recur on the same days of the month; (2) those days of the month too would fall usually on the same days of the week, and in any case not more than one day apart; for in 95 years we have (after the 52 weeks in each year) 95 extra days, and 23 or 24 leap-years each with a further day; in all 118 or 119 days; and as the chances are three to one that in 95 years there will be 24 leap-years, they are also three to one in favour of the larger number 119 days, or exactly seventeen weeks. Thus after 95 years, three times out of four, the full moon falling not only on the same day of the month but on the same day of the week, Easter, too, will fall the same number of days after it, that is, also on the same day of the month. Now if we want to find all possible Easters, say between A.D. 325 and 700, which fell on April 24, we turn to a cycle of 95 years and look for all Easters on that day or on one day each way—April 23, 24, 25—secure that further variation is impossible. In Dionysius' cycle there are only four such Easters. In A.D. 539 Easter fell on April 24; therefore on the same or next day in A.D. 349, *444*, 634. In A.D. 550 again on April 24; so A.D. *360*, 455, 645. In A.D. 577 on April 25: compare A.D. 387, 482, *672*. In A.D. 607 on April 23; compare A.D. 417, *512*. But of all these occasions only the four italicized years were leap-years; and all others are *ex hypothesi* excluded. Hence only A.D. 360, 444, 512, 672 can come into account. Now in A.D. 360 Easter fell on April 23, according to the Festal Letter of St. Athanasius for that year (see tables in Larsow's edition). In A.D. 444 it fell again on the same day, as stated by Proterius of Alexandria in his letter to Leo of Rome eleven years later (Migne, vol. 67, p. 510). In A.D. 512 it must have fallen on April 22; for the cycle of Dionysius commences in the next year with an Easter Sunday on April 7. And in A.D. 672 it certainly fell on April 25; see Ussher inf. There is therefore no single year which fulfils the conditions of Easter Sunday on April 24 in leap-year; and we may confidently conclude that even if the leap-year day was intercalated after April, at least the year of our Homilist was not leap-year, and in that case the normal equivalents between the Asiatic and Julian Kalendars must hold. *The full moon of the Homilist can only have fallen on April* 18, *and his Easter Day on April* 25.

But Ussher gives only four occasions between A.D. 140 and 919 on which Easter Sunday fell on the 25th of April, namely, the years

A. D. 387, 482, 577, 672. We will now put side by side our Homilist's four Easter dates in his own Asiatic months; then the ordinary equivalents of these in Roman months; and lastly the four sets of Easters (taken from Ussher, l. c. p. 1229) to one of which the Homily must certainly apply—

| | | | |
|---|---|---|---|
| 2nd day of 8th month | April 25 | A.D. 387.<br>482.<br>577.<br>672. | April 25<br>April 25<br>April 25<br>April 25 |
| 17th day of 7th month | April 9 | 388.<br>483.<br>578.<br>673. | April 9<br>April 10<br>April 10<br>April 10 |
| 9th day of 7th month | April 1 | 389.<br>484.<br>579.<br>674. | April 1<br>April 1<br>April 2<br>April 2 |
| 29th day of 7th month | April 21 | 390.<br>485.<br>580.<br>675. | April 21<br>April 21<br>April 21<br>April 22 |

Now of the four dates given in the Homily three must of course be reckoned by the ordinary Roman equivalents, for leap-year can only affect one in four. But no less than three of the four refuse to tally with the quartet A. D. 672–675, and two with the quartet A. D. 577–580. In the third set A. D. 482–485, only one year, it is true, differs; but this one, A. D. 483, is not leap-year. We conclude that the four years of the Homily must be the remaining quartet, A. D. 387–390, and here the correspondence is exact. Even in A. D. 388, the leap-year of the four, the Asiatic and Julian equivalents are for April 9 the same as in ordinary years; and consequently the Asiatic leap-year intercalation must have been made before the month in which this day occurs.

(4) It is strictly speaking superfluous, but at the same time it will add interest to the discussion and cogency to the conclusion if finally, as the coping-stone of the present argument, we can show that our Homily, now dated independently at A. D. 387, does in fact fit admirably into the historical conditions of that year and of the Paschal disputes which marked it. Till that year, Easter had not fallen as late as April 25 since the sub-Apostolic age, and it would preeminently be such a first occasion which would excite the opposition and alarm depicted in our Homily; while

before Easter fell again so late (A. D. 482) Alexandrine calculations were accepted as a matter of course in the East, and even at Rome they were largely introduced by Victorius about the middle of the fifth century, and fully by Dionysius Exiguus in the first half of the sixth. Again, appeal is made, as we said, to 'witnesses of good memory' for Easter falling after the 21st, while objectors admit Easter on the 21st but nothing more. Now Easter as a matter of fact had fallen on April 21 only eight years before, in A. D. 379; but before April 21, it had only fallen twice within sixty years—in A. D. 349 on April 23, and in A. D. 360 on the same day—and on the first of these occasions the Alexandrines, Athanasius being then on intimate terms with the Westerns and especially with the Roman See, yielded to the Roman earlier computation [1]. One instance within living memory, and that twenty-seven years before, would satisfy the contradictory assertions hazarded on the two sides.

Further we do know that in A. D. 387 the unusual lateness of the Alexandrine Easter aroused keen discussion, in which the Emperor Theodosius, with the view of reconciling the West to the Eastern practice, intervened. There is still extant the preface of a document addressed to him by Theophilus of Alexandria, whom he had consulted, as well as a circular letter which St. Ambrose from the same point of view directed to the bishops of Emilia.

Theophilus[2] writes that according to the Old Testament the month of the Passover was to be the first month or month of new year's produce ($\mu\grave{\eta}\nu\ \tau\hat{\omega}\nu\ \nu\acute{\epsilon}\omega\nu$) when the crops were full-grown; and the day to be the 14th, that is full moon, for the Jewish month, unlike the ancient Egyptian but like the Greek, was lunar. This month itself should be fixed after the equinox, which falls on the 25th Phamenoth, 21st of March, or according to the 'Syrians, Antiochenes, and Macedonians' 21st of Dystrus; if the previous (twelfth) month were to be taken, it would be found that the crops were not ready to cut. But when, the month being rightly fixed, its 14th falls on Sunday, Easter must be put off a week; for we may neither end our fast on the 13th nor yet fast on the Sunday—a thing no one would do but a Manichee[3]—while

---

[1] Cf. Hefele, *Councils*, E. T. ii. 159. The Easters during the Episcopate of Athanasius (A. D. 328-373) are given in Larsow's edition of the *Festal Letters*, p. 47.

[2] Ap. Gallandi, vii. 614.

[3] Μανιχαίων γὰρ ἴδιον πρᾶγμα τὸ τοιοῦτον.

on the contrary, as the Lord was crucified on the 14th[1], and therefore the Resurrection fell after it then, so may its Paschal commemoration now. As to objections on the score of lateness (of April 25), why the Law itself says, if you cannot keep the Passover in the first month, do so in the second; in any case therefore it is better to have Easter too late than too early.

St. Ambrose is addressing the bishops of Emilia, after the bishops of Rome and Alexandria had expressed their opinion, and apparently with Theophilus' epistle in his hands[2]. The Nicene fathers, he says, had instituted a nineteen years' cycle (after which the same dates for full moons were to recur) in order to secure unanimity about the night on which the 'sacrifice for the Lord's Resurrection' was to be offered[3]. We are to note the first month or month of new crops, and the 14th of the month; for Christ, coming to fulfil the Law of Moses, kept the Passover on the 14th (Thursday), being crucified on the 15th, and rising from the dead on the 17th. Thus the 14th as preceding the Passion, and therefore a fast, cannot be Easter day, which if the 14th is a Sunday —'sicut futurum est proxime'—will fall a week later, and in this case will be kept on the 25th, not on the 18th, of April. So, to quote recent practice, in A.D. 373[4] the 14th of the moon fell on March 24, and Easter a week later; in A.D. 377 the 14th was on April 9, and again Easter on the 16th.

But then, continues Ambrose, the objection is made that if

[1] Τῇ τεσσαρεσκαιδεκαταίᾳ in the Greek: but the Latin 'decimaquinta,' cf. Ambrose inf. and note 2 on p. 136.

[2] *Ambrosii Opera* (Venice, 1751), iii. pp. 935-943. 'Post Aegyptiorum supputationes et Alexandrinae Ecclesiae definitores, Episcopi quoque Romanae ecclesiae, per litteras plerique meam adhuc expectant sententiam'; elsewhere again, 'Alexandrini quoque et Aegyptii, ut ipsi scripserunt.' Further, he not only employs the Egyptian names of months, but presents actual coincidences with Theophilus' preface just mentioned, in the 'mensis novorum' and the reference to the Manichees.

On the important position held by the see of Milan at the end of the fourth century, see Duchesne, pp. 32-39.

[3] If the Gentiles observe days—'quintam esse fugiendam,' 'posteros dies vel Aegyptiacos declinare'—they do it for superstitious motives; we in order that 'consona sacrae noctis fundatur oratio.'

[4] St. Ambrose dates the years here by the era of Diocletian, the 89th and the 93rd. This era, specially made for Egypt, and continuously in use in the Coptic Church as the 'era of martyrs,' is reckoned from A.D. 284, the year of Diocletian's accession, and as the Egyptian year commenced on August 29, the 89th and 93rd year of the era will refer to the Easters not of A.D. 372 and 376, but of A.D. 373 and 377. Even the months Phamenoth and Pharmuthi are given as well as the Roman reckoning.

Easter is kept as late as April 25, the rule of the 'first month' is not observed. We answer—

(1) Since the full moon can obviously fall anywhere within the first solar month, if it falls quite at the end, then Easter, unless kept on the actual 14th, must fall in the next month.

(2) In the present case it is the Jews who will not observe the first month; for their Passover is to be on March 20, which belongs to the 12th month and not to the 1st[1], whether you reckon the latter as the post-equinoctial month of 31 days, from March 22 to April 21, or the Egyptian month Pharmuthi, of 30 days, from March 27 to April 25.

(3) But in reality, as scholars of the Jewish law know well, this first month is lunar; and if the first full moon after the equinox falls (as in A.D. 387) on April 18 the first new moon will fall on April 5, the nones of April[2], and the second therefore about the nones of May, so that April 25 falls well before it.

Moreover only two years ago Easter was celebrated as late as the 11th before the Kalends of May, the 30th of the (post-equinoctial) month[3], and the few extra days between that day and the 25th of April now proposed, ought not to be a real stumbling-block.

It is sufficiently obvious that the arguments of St. Ambrose and of Theophilus are in the main identical with those employed by our Homilist, and there can be no reasonable doubt that the three

---

[1] In Milan, the eighth month, 'octavus secundum consuetudinem nostram, indictio enim Septembri mense incipit, octavo igitur mense Kalendae Apriles sunt.'

[2] Such seems to be the meaning of the words 'cum a pluribus nonis lunae cursus incipiat, hoc est, dies primus, vides nonas Maii adhuc ad mensem primum novorum computari posse': where for 'a pluribus nonis' I suspect we should read 'Aprilibus Nonis.'

[3] 'Ante biennium celebraverimus paschae Dominicam undecimo Kalendas Maii, hoc est, trigesimo die mensis secundum nostram scilicet calculationem.' These figures do not seem to tally; a. d. xi Kal. Mai. is April 21, but the 30th of a month commencing on March 22 would be April 20: so for 'trigesimo' we ought perhaps to restore 'triges[imo pr]imo.' If April 21 is thus correct, the nearest year given in the tables in which Easter fell on that day is A.D. 379; and as on the other hand it seems probable (e. g. from the repeated use of 'proxime') that the letter was not written very long before the Easter of A.D. 387, it has been proposed to read 'ante vi ennium' (i. e. sexennium) for 'ante biennium.' [I do not know whether it is possible that in A.D. 384 the full moon which fell about March 21 may have been reckoned in Milan as before the equinox, so that the Paschal moon would fall about April 19, and Easter day, instead of on March 24, on April 21.]

writers refer to the same occasion. By concurrent but independent lines of argument it has therefore been established that the four Easters of the Homily are those from A. D. 387 to 390; and if so, then (as we have seen) the date given for the leap-year Easter of A. D. 388 shows that the intercalation was made before Easter and before the month beginning on March 24. It was already argued in the main body of this Essay (p. 122, sup.), that the intercalation probably did take place in the sixth Asiatic month (Feb. 21 to March 23) in Asia as in Rome. So far therefore from demonstrating an alternative theory to be correct, the Paschal Homily is absolutely consistent, so far as it goes, with the theory of intercalation on which this Essay is based[1].

## APPENDIX II.

## PASSAGES FROM ANCIENT WRITERS WHO EMPLOY KALENDARS OF THE ASIATIC TYPE, GIVING SIDE BY SIDE A ROMAN AND A NATIVE DATING.

### [C. H. T.]

Dr. Lightfoot has quoted (Ignatius i. 665) four inscriptions which give side by side the two methods of dating. For completeness' sake I have put together here the few instances which are quoted by Archbishop Ussher from ancient writers.

1. Epiphanius, *Haeres.* 51. § 24. The Baptism of Christ, κατ' Αἰγυπτίους Ἀθὺρ δωδεκάτῃ πρὸ ἓξ εἰδῶν Νοεμβρίων, κατὰ Ἕλληνας Δίου ὀγδόῃ . . . . κατὰ Παφίους Ἀπογονικοῦ ἑκκαιδεκάτῃ . . . . κατὰ Μακεδόνας Ἀπελλαίου ἑκκαιδεκάτῃ.

---

[1] Of course (I repeat what I have said before) the correctness of this theory of intercalation does not prove that St. Polycarp suffered in A D. 156 and not in A. D. 155. That he did suffer in the later year is made possible by it, and the possible becomes probable, if once the identification of the 'high sabbath' with the Purim feast is admitted.

150     *Passages from Ancient Writers*

Here the date intended is of course Nov. 8, and the Asiatic or, as Epiphanius here calls it, the 'Macedonian' date, Apellaeus 16, is correctly given according to the Hemerology; for Apellaeus commences a. d. ix Kal. Nov. (Oct. 24) and does not repeat its first. But a second kalendar on the Asiatic model was the Cyprian, as the Hemerology calls it, or as Epiphanius calls it (to distinguish it from the Kalendar of Salamis) the Paphian; and the Paphian date is again correctly given as Apogonicus 16.

2. Epiphanius, *ib.* The Birth of Christ, πρὸ ὀκτὼ εἰδῶν 'Ιανουαρίων . . . κατ' Αἰγυπτίους Τυβὶ ἐνδεκάτῃ, κατὰ Σύρους εἴτ' οὖν ˝Ελληνας Αὐδυναίου ἕκτῃ . . . . . κατὰ Παφίους 'Ιουλίου τεσσαρεσκαιδεκάτῃ. The date meant is January 6, and the 'Asiatic' date is not among the parallels here given (but cf. the Paschal Homily, p. 142, sup.): however the Paphian date recurs, and we learn (as indeed the Hemerology would tell us) that the Paphian months, though all beginning like the Asiatic months on a. d. ix Kal., did not repeat the first in months of 31 days. For 'Julius' begins a. d. ix Kal. Jan. (Dec. 24) and if it repeated its first the 14th would have been Jan. 7, not Jan. 6.

3. The panegyric entitled *Laudatio S. Barnabae Apostoli* written by a certain Alexander, a monk of Cyprus, and printed in the *Acta Sanctorum* for June 11 (June, tom. ii. pp. 431–447) gives St. Barnabas' day as κατὰ μὲν 'Ρωμαίοις τῇ πρὸ τριῶν εἰδῶν 'Ιουνίων, κατὰ δὲ Κυπρίους Κωνσταντιεῖς μηνὸς Μεσωρεί, τοῦ καὶ δεκάτου, ιαʹ, κατὰ δὲ 'Ασιανοὺς ἤτοι κατὰ Παφίους Πληθυπάτου τοῦ καὶ ἐννάτου ιθʹ. The ninth 'Asiatic or Paphian' month, commencing a. d. ix Kal. Jun. (May 24) and not repeating its first, will make its 19th on June 11; but Plethypatus is, strictly speaking, only a Paphian and not an Asiatic name (Lightfoot, i. p. 682).

The rough date of this little panegyric is easily fixed; for it discusses the history of Peter the Fuller bishop of Antioch and his claim over Cyprus, so opportunely met by the discovery of the relics of St. Barnabas, and must therefore be later than A.D. 480, while it obviously precedes the Saracen invasions of Cyprus, and must therefore be earlier than A.D. 650. But since Alexander speaks of the Theopaschite addition to the Trisagion made by Peter, ὁ σταυρωθεὶς δι' ἡμᾶς, as still largely in use in his own day among the more simple-minded orthodox, I should conclude that this writing must belong to the earlier half of the sixth century. (See Dict. Christ. Ant. s.v. Trisagion: Bingham, book xiv. ch. 2,

§ 3). Photius (cod. 228) preserves an account of a letter written by Ephraimius, Patriarch of Antioch from about A. D. 527 to 547, in which he maintains the orthodoxy both of the Easterns who used the addition (addressing the hymn to Christ) and the Westerns or Byzantines who rejected it on the ground that the hymn was really addressed to the Holy Trinity. But after this there does not seem to be any mention of the enlarged Trisagion at least in orthodox circles.

4. In the Acts of Timothy (printed in the *Acta Sanctorum*, January, ii. p. 566) the saint is said to have been martyred 'in nefanda festivitate eorum, quam vocabant Catagogicrum, quae est secundum Asianos quidem mensis quarti die tricesima, secundum autem Romanos mensis Januarii vicesima secunda.' The fourth month commenced a. d. ix Kal. Dec. (Dec. 24) and being a month of 31 days, should repeat the first, so that the Asiatic 30th ought to be Jan. 23 not Jan. 22. It is possible therefore that at some unknown date the system of the double first was dropped, and the days in all months counted straight through, so that the Asiatic Kalendar was in fact assimilated to the Paphian Kalendar described above, in which Jan. 22 would be the 30th of the 4th month. This may be the reason why Alexander the monk, as we saw, can quote a date as κατὰ δὲ 'Ασιανοὺς ἤτοι κατὰ Παφίους. Unfortunately there is nothing on the face of these Acts of Timothy to fix their date; but they were read by Photius (cod. 254), while, on the other hand, the application of the title Patriarch to the Bishop of Ephesus seems to show that they are not earlier than A. D. 450. [Prof. Sanday now kindly informs me that Usener, in his edition of these Acts (which I was unable to find in the Bodleian) and Schürer, in reviewing Usener, both fix on a date some time in the fourth century; I should scarcely have thought they were so early.]

---

NOTE.—ON THE NEW MATTER CONTAINED IN THE SECOND EDITION (1889), OF BISHOP LIGHTFOOT'S APOSTOLIC FATHERS, (PART II. ST. IGNATIUS, ST. POLYCARP, VOL. I. pp. 626–722).

[This edition appeared when the proof of the preceding paper had all but finally left my hands, and I am therefore unable to do more than add the present note, calling attention to the chief additions to the discussion on St. Polycarp's martyrdom. These, so far as a rapid glance enables one to judge, seem to be mainly the following:—

(*a*) On p. 683 (ed. i. p. 666), a sentence is added on the inscription from Ephesus, for which cf. p. 120 sup.

(*b*) On p. 687 an unpublished Pergamene inscription, communicated by Mommsen, is printed so far as it bears on the Asiatic Kalendar.

(*c*) On p. 714 *n*. (ed. i. p. 696), the judgment on Usener's theory of the term Σεβαστή is reworded.

(*d*) On p. 727, Dr. Lightfoot is good enough to discuss the theory offered in the preceding pages. The Bishop of Salisbury (through Prof. Sanday) had kindly asked the present writer to send him a note on the date of the martyrdom, and this was printed in the new edition of the late Bishop of Lincoln's *Church History*. In this shape it has come under the notice of Dr. Lightfoot, who criticises its theory of leap-year intercalation, on the ground that the intercalated day must have been the same in Asia as in Rome. This may be so, though Archbishop Ussher, as we have seen, placed it at nearly six months' distance instead of only two days. The last few lines of the Bishop's criticism (where '3rd Xanthicus' occurs three times in mistake, I think, for 2nd Xanthicus) show that I did not succeed in making myself intelligible in the limits of a short abstract. I hope I may have been more fortunate in the preceding paper. C. H. T.]

The inscription from Pergamon (p. 687) is of considerable interest. It is a dedication to Hadrian by a religious college, and names the days annually to be celebrated by the three officials of the corporation. The kalendar employed is obviously Asiatic, for the names Lous, Panemus, Peritius, Hyperberetaeus, occur for various months, and the birthday of Hadrian (a. d. ix Kal. Feb. = Jan. 24) falls on the Σεβαστή or first[1] of the month Καῖσαρ, the latter name being apparently substituted for Dystrus (Jan. 24—Feb. 20) in honour of the reigning Emperor[2]. The curious

---

[1] Usener's theory on this point, accepted above (p. 121), is now admitted by Dr. Lightfoot to be probable (p. 714 *n*.).

[2] It is true that the Cypriot (Paphian) Kalendar, dating from the time of Augustus, already used Caesarius for this same month; but the Ephesian Caesarius was a different month, September–October, so called obviously from the birthday of Augustus.

coincidence that the second of the two Emperors whose worship was most extravagantly practised in Asia had his birthday, like the first, on a. d. ix Kal., must have given considerable impetus to a kalendar whose ruling principle was the celebration of this Emperor's day on the first of each month. Further, we find in this inscription that in both the months Panemus and Lous, the three officials observe respectively the days Σεβ, β', γ', that is most naturally the 1st, 2nd, 3rd. Now Lous, as a month of 31 days, ought to have repeated its first, so that the three days would be Σεβ, α', β'; and there is therefore a possibility that at Pergamon in Hadrian's time, the double first was not in use, the days being numbered from 1 to 31, which would bring the Pergamene Kalendar into exact agreement with those of Bithynia, Crete and Cyprus (see Lightfoot, p. 681, and for Cyprus, or more properly Paphos, sup. p. 150), all of them different from the Asiatic on this point. A similar kalendar was in use at Attalia in Pamphylia in the third century[1], whither it no doubt travelled direct from Paphos. In Proconsular Asia itself the compiler of the (late) Acts of Timothy, presumably an Ephesian, omitted the doubled first (sup. p. 151). This alteration Dr. Lightfoot now supposes to have been made at an early date, explaining his second inscription—that from Ephesus of A. D. 104, where, as we saw (p. 120 sup.), Anthesterion or Xanthicus 2 is Feb. 22, not Feb. 23 —on these lines; 'the inconvenience of reckoning two first days must have been seriously felt and would eventually lead to the substitution of another nomenclature at this point without destroying the general framework of the kalendar' (p. 683). Only in the first place, if all this is so, there is no antecedent reason why the 2nd Xanthicus of St. Polycarp's martyrdom fifty years later may not also be an instance where the double first has been dropped, so that the equivalent date would again be Feb. 22, not Feb. 23. It is true that this suggestion implies that the equation in the extant text (a. d. vii Kal. Mart. Feb. 23) is incorrect; but there is certainly no positive objection to treating the Roman date as a later insertion for the benefit of non-Asiatic readers, and since *ex hypothesi* both the use and the omission of the double first were current in Asia, there is nothing strange if of the two interpretations of Xanthicus 2 (Feb. 22 and 23), a later writer adopted

---

[1] Lightfoot, p. 684, μηνὶ η', κβ' ἕως λα', τῶν ι' ἡμερῶν, equated to May 14-23.

one as most familiar to himself, while it was the other which really corresponded to the original date.

As a matter of fact the reckoning of the double first did in fact survive long after the second century, as has been shown in the appendix from the use of the Asiatic Kalendar in Pseudo-Chrysostom. The martyrdom of Pionius (Lightfoot, i. 720), obviously depends on it also, for the 12th March is there the 19th of the Asiatic month. On the other hand, of the authorities quoted against the double first, the Pamphylian inscription is too far removed in place, and the Acts of Timothy in time. Then the Pergamene inscription on closer examination shows signs of Asiatic structure; the last but one of the month is still denoted $\pi\rho\bar{o}$, and this means that the last ten days of the month were reckoned backwards, as in the Asiatic Kalendar, and in it only. If an assimilation to the Bithynian and Cyprian type had taken place, the double first would indeed have disappeared, but the backward counting of ten days (which would now have become eleven days) would probably have been dropped for simple enumeration from 1 to 31. Moreover, it is not easy to believe that within the limits of so small an area as Proconsular Asia two kalendars so like, and yet so unlike (for the change would alter by one day at least 140 days in the year), prevailed side by side. That the system of the double first existed, we know; that the contrary system also existed is not *proved* by the Pergamene inscription; and the Ephesian inscription, though compatible with it, is equally compatible with the hypothesis here suggested.

It was on the assumption that only one kalendar was in use, and in order to meet the two objections as to the pontificate of Anicetus and the high sabbath of Purim in connection with the earlier year, that Feb. 22, A. D. 156 was offered in this paper as a possible alternative to Feb. 23, A. D. 155. Dr. Lightfoot now says (p. 727), that he does not 'lay any stress on this particular solution' of the high sabbath, although he still seems to prefer it[1]; and he is arguing, he tells us, in his forthcoming edition of St. Clement, that 'it is impossible with our existing data to fix the accessions of the Roman bishops in the middle of the second

---

[1] Dr. Lightfoot adds that 'whether in this age the Jews intercalated by whole months or by fractions of months, we cannot say': I should have thought it impossible for a lunar kalendar to intercalate less than a complete moon.

century within three or four years, though a strict reckoning would suggest A. D. 153–155 for that of Anicetus': if the first of these alternative years A. D. 153 is the true one, then the visit of Polycarp can be placed in A. D. 154, and the martyrdom early in the following year. Undoubtedly if another identification than Purim can be found for the high sabbath which will suit Feb. 23, A. D. 155; and if the accession of Anicetus can be placed as early as Dr. Lightfoot believes; and if two kalendars were simultaneously in use in Proconsular Asia; the ground is cut away from any theory such as that here presented which based itself on the explanation of the 'high sabbath' selected by Dr. Lightfoot himself, and on the chronological difficulty raised by Prof. Lipsius, the writer who had up to that time devoted most study to the episcopal successions at Rome. But until these points are satisfactorily settled there may be something to be said for the date suggested in this paper.

www.ingramcontent.com/pod-product-compliance
Lightning Source LLC
Chambersburg PA
CBHW032007220426
43664CB00005B/171